METRO BOOKS
New York

An Imprint of Sterling Publishing Co., Inc.
1166 Avenue of the Americas
New York, NY 10036

ISBN 978-1-4351-6252-5

For information about custom editions, special sales, and
premium and corporate purchases, please contact
Sterling Special Sales at 800-805-5489
or specialsales@sterlingpublishing.com.

Manufactured in China

2 4 6 8 10 9 7 5 3 1

www.sterlingpublishing.com

Design and illustration by Michael Lebihan

Conceived, designed, and produced by
Quid Publishing
Part of The Quarto Group
Level 4 Sheridan House
114 Western Road
Hove BN3 1DD
England

www.quidpublishing.com

UNSOLVED

MYSTERIES

BIZARRE EVENTS THAT HAVE PUZZLED THE GREATEST MINDS

JOEL LEVY

METRO BOOKS
New York

CONTENTS

INTRODUCTION

The craving for mystery tells us something profound about the human condition. Humans have evolved to be storytellers, pattern-finders, problem-solvers; our psychology, the very wiring of our brains, is set up to construct narratives and find explanations. This is why curiosity drives us all, from little children at play to scientists exploring the universe. Solving puzzles is satisfying, whether it be the morning crossword or the operation of fundamental forces. Yet still we are fascinated by mysteries: we seek them out and obsess over them; we often prefer that they remain unsolved.

Perhaps the explanation for this contradictory craving can be glimpsed in the tension that lies at the heart of mystery. A mystery is a puzzle that might have a solution, a secret that could be revealed—it is a legend, but with a kernel of truth. Mystery offers the potential for answers, yet the tension between enigma and explanation remains unresolved.

"Apart from the known and the unknown," asks a character in Harold Pinter's play *The Homecoming*, "what else is there?" Mysteries sit at the border between these two categories, a liminal zone between disciplines and worlds. A true mystery has an X-factor that lifts it above the status of an unanswered question or unsolved puzzle. The mysteries in this book display this indefinable quality; they exist in the twilight zone where mysteries come alive: where fact meets fiction, the natural meets the supernatural, and the normal meets the paranormal.

The cases in these pages resist simple classification, partly by virtue of being mysterious, but they are organized nonetheless into four broad categories: Mysterious Places; Unsolved Events; Strange Sightings; and Cryptic Artifacts. The first category, Mysterious Places, explores enigmas associated with particular locations which are themselves enigmatic. Unsolved Events mainly details human mysteries, especially unexplained disappearances. Strange Sightings covers bizarre encounters and weird experiences. Cryptic Artifacts looks at strange objects and technology out of time and place.

Left: Easter Island moai; colossal stone busts that guard the many mysteries of Easter Island and its lost culture.

determine how or even whether he was murdered, let alone who did it; decipher the mysterious code associated with him; or discover why he carried a cryptic Persian message. The case is almost the inverse of a mysterious disappearance: a man's body has appeared, but everything that might be known about him remains just out of reach, although there are tantalizing hints of Cold War espionage and a secret love child.

Inevitably some of the categories are loosely defined, partly in order to accommodate mysteries that refuse to fit nicely into a straightforward classification. Take, for instance, the Tamam Shud case, in which a corpse was found on an Australian beach in 1948, bearing a peculiar, encoded note. It remains impossible to identify the dead man;

Like all the best mysteries, the Tamam Shud case remains unexplained and probably insoluble. In other cases I have tried, where possible, to point to likely solutions to each enigma, but it is these enduring mysteries that are the most attractive. In the words of Albert Einstein, "the most beautiful thing we can experience is the mysterious."

MYSTERIOUS PLACES

A place need not be real to be mysterious; the mythical lost continent of Atlantis probably never existed beyond the mind of the ancient Greek philosopher Plato, yet it has inspired an entire industry of speculation and investigation. Stonehenge on the other hand is very real, and although it is one of the most closely scrutinized prehistoric monuments in the world, it continues to offer up fresh mysteries. In December 2015 investigators announced the discovery of one of the actual quarries from where the Stonehenge bluestones originated, only to learn that they had been quarried some 500 years before their erection at Stonehenge. This raises the intriguing possibility that Stonehenge itself is a copy or reinterpretation of a much older monument originally erected somewhere in Wales.

Other prehistoric sites haunt our collective imagination, from the landscape-spanning glyphs of the Nasca Lines to the brooding colossi of Easter Island. How were these extraordinary monuments constructed and what did they mean? A different set of questions attaches to the putative locations of lost treasures and great secrets, such as the fabled El Dorado, kingdom of gold, the ornate symbolism of Rosslyn Chapel, the tall tales of the Oak Island Money Pit, and the sacred landscape and obscure occultism of Rennes-le-Château. What riches might lie hidden at these locations, and what earth-shattering revelations might they yet conceal?

Left: The trilithons of Stonehenge at sunrise, around the time of the summer solstice.

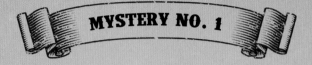

ATLANTIS

Date: 9600 BCE
Location: Beyond the Straits of Hercules

Plato's tale, supposedly of ancient Egyptian origin, tells of a lost island empire in the Atlantic, believed later by pseudo-historians and mystics to be the cradle of all civilization.

Atlantis was a great island beyond the Straits of Hercules, home to a rich and glorious kingdom that became an empire, before perishing in a flood sent as divine punishment for hubris and corruption. Since Plato first told this tale 2,500 years ago, Atlantis has been imagined in every corner of the globe and ascribed mystical attributes from telepathy to flying cars. It has become a repository for every aspect of New Age thought and alternative history supposition, from Hollow Earth flying saucers to environmental doomsday prophecies.

The original source for Atlantis is the writing of the ancient Athenian philosopher Plato. In two dialogues, *Timaeus* and *Critias*, probably written in the mid-4th century BCE, Plato explains that the story had come to him via a chain of descent from the ancient Athenian poet, statesman, and lawgiver Solon.

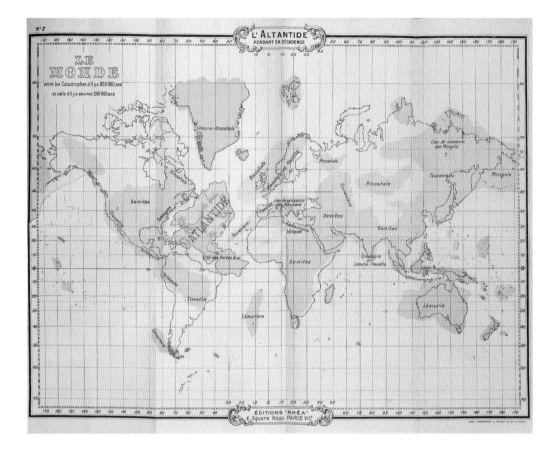

While traveling in Egypt in 590 BCE, an Egyptian priest had shown Solon a column upon which the tale was recorded—a tale of incredible antiquity, which Plato clearly dates to 9,000 years earlier (i.e. around 9600 BCE). Right from the start of Plato's detailed account, he makes clear the size and position of Atlantis:

> *This power* [Atlantis] *came forth out of the Atlantic Ocean, for in those days the Atlantic was navigable; and there was an island situated in front of the straits which are by you called the Pillars of Hercules; the island was greater than Libya* [i.e. northern Africa] *and Asia* [i.e. modern-day Turkey and the Near East] *put together . . .*

Above: A map from William Scott Elliot's 1896 *The Story of Atlantis*, showing the landmasses of the world in the era of Atlantis, as revealed by clairvoyance.

PLATO'S ATLANTIS

Plato describes a huge island ringed with mountains, with a capital city (also called Atlantis) in the center of a plain, ringed with concentric canals and great walls. At its center was a rocky hill bearing a temple to Poseidon, the sea god and creator of the kingdom. Though gifted with all the earthly and human gifts imaginable, including natural bounty, rich mineral wealth, powerful armies, and great wisdom and learning, Atlantis grew greedy and overbearing. Her armies conquered deep into Africa and threatened Europe, resisted only by brave Athens, until Poseidon grew angry and visited destruction upon the land he had created: "There occurred violent earthquakes and floods; and in a single day and night of misfortune . . . the island of Atlantis . . . disappeared in the depths of the sea. For which reason the sea in those parts is impassable and impenetrable, because there is a shoal of mud in the way; and this was caused by the subsidence of the island."

Opposite: Rock art from *ca.* 6500 BCE; evidence like this suggests that the Bronze Age technology described by Plato had not yet emerged in the 10th millennium BCE.

Below: A classic Romantic depiction of the collapse of civilization, a theme epitomized in the tale of Atlantis.

Plato's tale is dramatic and detailed, but without evidence. He places Atlantis in the 10th millennium BCE—near the start of the Neolithic era in conventional history, when agriculture was just beginning. People lived in small groups, rarely settled for long, built small, perishable structures, and used stone, wood, bone, and antler. Yet the Atlantis and Athens described by Plato are clearly high Bronze Age societies, with bronze arms and armor, ocean-going ships, great cities, and monumental architecture. There is no conventionally accepted evidence of a civilization even approaching the level described by Plato until the 4th millennium BCE at the earliest.

BEFORE THE FLOOD

But what if the evidence is all around us, if we have but the wit to see it? In the 19th century, Atlantology (the study of Atlantis) significantly evolved to what might be called the proto-scientific stage, in which Atlantis scholars sought to bring together contemporary fashions in science, archaeology, and anthropology. Proto-scientific Atlantology was the brainchild of American politician, journalist, and amateur historian Ignatius Donnelly, whose 1882 book *Atlantis: The Antediluvian World* was a massive bestseller and radically transformed perceptions of Atlantis forever.

Donnelly saw the evidence for Atlantis in similarities between distant cultures. Why did civilizations on either side of the Atlantic share features such as pyramid-building, sun worship, and myths about great floods, he wondered. Donnelly argued that they all shared a common source: an original or Ur-civilization from which all others had sprung, either through colonization or relocation after natural disaster. This theory, known as diffusionism, still forms the central tenet of much pseudo-history and Atlantology today. Like Plato, Donnelly located this original civilization in the Atlantic Ocean, pointing to the Azores and Canaries, and the great undersea mountains recently discovered by oceanography expeditions as remnants of a lost continent which had sunk in cataclysmic events of the type then current in geological thought.

REVISIONIST ATLANTOLOGY

It is now known that the ocean floor is dense basalt, while the rocks that make up the continental landmasses are relatively light and less dense, so it would be impossible for a continent to "sink" into the ocean, as Donnelly described. Geological advances have also shown that seamounts like the Azores and the Canaries are not remnants of sunken continents but volcanic mountains created by local hotspots of magma welling up through the ocean floor.

Proto-scientific Atlantology gave way to a new stage: revisionist Atlantology, which argues that Plato's account is not to be taken literally, but refers to a prehistoric super-civilization unknown to present-day historians. Atlantologists have since sought Atlantis in almost every corner of the globe. Amongst many contenders, one of the most notable revisionist candidates is the Minoan settlement on Thera (now Santorini) in the Mediterranean, destroyed by a colossal volcanic eruption in around 1500 BCE.

The most plausible reading of Plato's Atlantis, however, is that he made it up. For inspiration, Plato needed look no further than Helike, about 100 miles (160 km) to the west of Athens, which in 373 BCE was submerged by a huge earthquake and tsunami. Helike had been leader of the powerful Achaean League, with a great temple to Poseidon. It disappeared, literally overnight, when Plato was about 54, and it seems inconceivable that he did not think of it when writing about Atlantis around 17 years later.

— FAR OUT —
THEORIES

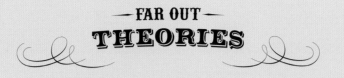

Donnelly's work coincided with the growing popularity of the mystical movement, notably theosophy, an eclectic blend of Oriental mysticism, spiritualism, and pseudo-science. Atlantis proved fertile territory for the mystical imagination, sparking the development of a new, mystical phase in Atlantology. Using methods such as astral travel, past-life memories, and communication with ethereal spirits, exciting new revelations about Atlantis and other lost continents poured forth. Atlantis became linked in the popular imagination with mastery of paranormal powers such as telepathy and occult technology like the use of a mystical energy called vril. In the 20th century this in turn spawned dark fantasies about Nazi-inflected alternative histories of Earth involving epic wars between master races and evil, degenerate races, in which Aryan demigods wielded vril-powered technologies (such as flying saucers) from their Atlantean utopia, until it was destroyed in a clash of civilizations. Today, many aspects of

Above: A Victorian tome on spiritualism, reflecting the burgeoning popularity of mysticism and the occult at the time.

this mystical Atlantology survive in contemporary New Age thought, with themes such as the survival of Atlantean spirits inside modern people, parallels between the "ecocide" of the ancient Atlanteans and modern capitalist–consumerist society, and the availability of Atlantean-style superpowers to those with the right sort of "vibrations."

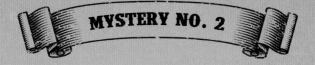

STONEHENGE

Date: 3ʳᵈ millennium BCE
Location: Salisbury Plain, Wiltshire, England

England's prehistoric megalithic stone circle and its intricately designed surroundings are ancient enigmas, that have long been shrouded in mystery regarding their purpose and construction.

Stonehenge is a complex prehistoric monument that includes concentric circles of standing stones, a ditch and bank, avenues, other earthworks and burial mounds, a ring of small pits, and other elements. It is part of a prehistoric landscape including many burial mounds, earthworks (particularly long avenues, or cursuses), and other henges of wood and stone, particularly the important site known as Durrington Walls, 2 miles (3.2 km) to the northeast of Stonehenge.

From the Middle Ages, Stonehenge appears in English legend through the work of the 12th-century romance writer Geoffrey of Monmouth and others, and in the Early Modern period (17th–18th centuries) it was the focus of some of the earliest antiquarian investigations in England. Medieval and Early Modern writers variously attributed its construction to the Romans, the

Druids, or the wizard Merlin (with the assistance of giants), but modern archaeology has revealed that it was built by the neolithic inhabitants of Britain. Stonehenge was constructed and rearranged in phases from around 3000 BCE to 2450 BCE, although the site continued to be used and modified long after this.

THE STONE GALLOWS

Today, the most striking feature of Stonehenge is the remains of a ring of tall sandstone "sarsens" around a horseshoe-shaped group of sarsens, some of which still stand as trilithons: pairs of uprights supporting lintel stones. This arrangement resembled the gallows of the medieval period, and this is the likely derivation of the name "henge" (from the Old English for "hanging" or "gallows"), so that Stonehenge meant "Stone Gallows." The monument gave its name to the whole class of megalithic circles, which are now called "henges" whether or not they include trilithons. Alongside

Below: Some of the massive trilithons of Stonehenge, which would once have formed a continuous circle of uprights and lintels.

the sarsen circles are the remnants of a partial ring of smaller "bluestones" (igneous rock that looks dark blue when freshly cut, wet, or polished). Within the circles is the Altar Stone, and around them are concentric rings of pits and holes, two burial mounds, and a set of four Station Stones arranged in a square, all enclosed by a circular ditch and bank. Leading off to the northeast are the remains of an avenue marked by earthen banks, sitting within which is the Heel Stone. But how was the site constructed, and what was its purpose?

Opposite: Plan views and elevations from an 1816 encyclopedia, showing contemporary Stonehenge and a speculative reconstruction.

MERLIN'S MAGIC OR GIANTS' MIGHT?

The sarsens are colossal rocks weighing, on average, 28 tons (25 tonnes), while the Heel Stone weighs 33 tons (30 tonnes). These sandstone blocks probably came from the Marlborough Downs, 20 miles (32 km) away. The bluestones come from the Preseli Hills in southwest Wales, and although they are smaller they still weigh 2.2–5.5 tons (2–5 tonnes) each. Transporting and erecting such heavy stones must have been tremendously difficult, and medieval authors ascribed the feat to supernatural agency.

Geoffrey of Monmouth imagined Merlin moving the stones from Ireland, using "gear" and skill, while the earliest known depiction of Stonehenge, from a manuscript of the 12th-century *Roman de Brut* (based on Geoffrey's work), shows Merlin directing giants as they lift the lintels into place.

In fact, reconstructions have shown that neolithic technology involving ropes, wooden frames, earthen ramps, mounds and ditches, and considerable muscle power can account for the erection of the monuments without recourse to supernatural or paranormal agency.

Below: A helpful giant constructing Stonehenge under Merlin's supervision, from a 12th-century illustrated manuscript.

—18—

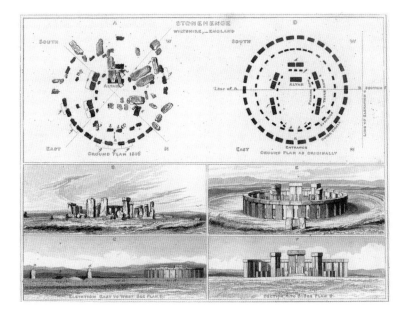

Nonetheless, transport of the bluestones from the Preseli Hills must have involved an epic sequence of river, sea, and overland transport, which expands modern appreciation of the capabilities and reach of neolithic peoples. One intriguing study by Oxford University landscape archaeologist Anthony Johnson suggests that neolithic architects could have employed sophisticated geometry to lay out the monument, using stakes, ropes, and straight edges, and demonstrating that "the builders of Stonehenge had a sophisticated yet empirically derived knowledge of Pythagorean geometry 2,000 years before Pythagoras."

PARTY ANIMALS

Constructing Stonehenge was a massive undertaking, so why was it done? Just as the site itself evolved over time, so it is likely that its function also changed. Early antiquarians thought that the monument was built by ancient Druids and assumed it was designed for Druidic ritual and sacrifice. Although almost nothing is known about these practices, modern Druid revivalists (aka neo-pagans) have adopted Stonehenge to stage major rituals. In fact, there is clear evidence that the site was still in use in the Iron Age and Roman times, so it is plausible that Druids did worship here, but that reveals nothing about the monument's original purpose.

Stonehenge is now thought to have been an ancient observatory or astronomical calculator. The monument seems to be aligned for the midwinter solstice, so processions approaching from the Avenue would see the midwinter sun setting directly over the focal altar stone. It may also have marked out lunar alignments: the Station Stones also line up with the southernmost moonrise of the Moon's 18-year cycle of movement along the horizon.

These alignments were almost certainly important, but may be supplementary to Stonehenge's main purpose. On this there are three main theories: it was a burial ground; a healing center (a "prehistoric Lourdes"); or the site of communal festivities. Human remains have been discovered at or around Stonehenge, such as the 50,000 cremated bone fragments from 63 different people buried in small pits around the stone circle, or the "Amesbury Archer," the high-status metal smith from the Alps found near neighboring Amesbury and sometimes described as "the king of Stonehenge." Such finds have prompted speculation that the site was a burial ground, or was used for ancestor worship or funeral rituals. Perhaps the large Avenue (a long trench-like earthwork) between Stonehenge and Durrington Walls served as a boundary between the realm of the dead (the stone circle) and that of the living (Durrington Walls). Many of the human remains show evidence of illness or deformity (the Amesbury Archer had suffered from a knee abscess for many years), while some of the bluestones show evidence that slivers were chipped off, possibly as curative talismans. So perhaps Stonehenge was a place people came to be healed; isotope analysis of bones associated with the site shows that people came from as far afield as the Mediterranean and the Alps to visit.

— FAR OUT — THEORIES

Stonehenge and other prehistoric monuments are integral to the New Age movement known as "earth mysteries," and specifically to theories about lines of force running through the landscape, popularly known as ley lines. Although ley line theory takes many forms, one version states that monuments such as henges were placed along lines of mystical earth energy perceptible to prehistoric peoples, serving both to mark their course and channel their energy. In this reading, Stonehenge is like a battery or charging station for earth energy, somehow making it accessible through now-forgotten technology or magic. Such theories have been incorporated

Above: Many solstice revelers visiting Stonehenge believe the stones channel mystic Earth energy.

into fantastical narratives about vril, a mystical energy available to Hollow Earth dwellers, Atlanteans from the ancient island empire of Atlantis (see page 10), and flying-saucer pilots.

Finds at Durrington Walls show that up to 4,000 people at a time gathered near Stonehenge, at a time when the population of Britain was possibly under 100,000. Animal bones show that they feasted, and the age of the animals shows that this occurred in winter. At least one of the animals was brought all the way from Scotland. So perhaps Stonehenge was associated with massive midwinter festivals, which may have provided the manpower for some of the labor-intensive works involved in altering the landscape.

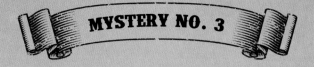

THE NASCA LINES

Date: *ca.* 500 BCE–*ca.* 700 CE
Location: Nasca Valley, Peru

Ancient lines drawn on the Peruvian desert 2,000 years ago form shapes and patterns described by UNESCO as "one of the most impenetrable enigmas of archaeology." But were they visible except from the air, and why were they created?

In 1926, Peruvian archaeologist Toribio Mejia Xesspe, hiking the hills around the arid Peruvian coastal plains, about 250 miles (400 km) south of Lima, spotted something remarkable on the hillsides and the pampas below. The outside world only became aware of this astonishing discovery when aircraft started to fly over the plains in the 1930s, and the existence of the Nasca lines, named for the Nasca or Nazca valley where they are most apparent, was revealed.

Technically known as geoglyphs ("earth drawings"), the lines come in diverse forms and patterns, found across a wide area of over 175 square miles (450 sq km), both on the pampas and in the surrounding foothills. They fall into two broad categories: pictures and lines. About 70 representational pictures have been identified, mainly biomorphs (animal shapes), including a few

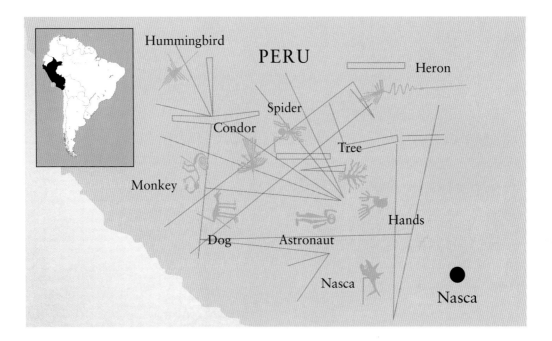

Above: A map showing the distribution of some of the most famous Nasca petroglyph figures and associated lines.

anthropomorphic shapes, and also some flowers, plants, trees, and everyday objects. The animals represented include killer whales, a spider, a monkey, a hummingbird, and the largest biomorph, a 935-foot (285-m) long pelican. The lines and geometric figures criss-cross the pampas and sometimes overlay one another. They can run in straight lines for up to several miles, but also form labyrinths and spirals, trapezoids, triangles, and rectangles. There are also "tracks" that seem to have been made to accommodate large groups of people.

The geoglyphs were made by taking advantage of the special conditions of the arid pampas, where the surface layer of iron-rich sand and gravel has acquired a dark patina through millennia of weathering. Clearing away the surface layer reveals the paler layers below, making it possible to draw in "negative" fashion. In most parts of the world the geoglyphs would quickly have been obscured and destroyed by weathering and land use, but the unique conditions of the coastal plains mean there is little wind or

Above: A collection of the most striking biomorphic Nasca glyphs.

rain, and few people, to damage the lines. The geoglyphs were made continuously over a long period from around 500 BCE up to around 700 CE. The earliest stage of their creation was during the Chavín period (*ca.* 1000–400 BCE), when simple figures were made by piling stones, followed by the Paracas period (*ca.* 900 BCE–400 CE) when a distinctive local culture grew up and created geoglyphs mainly on the hill slopes. The majority of the glyphs, including the finest biomorphs and the geometric figures and lines proper, date from the final period (*ca.* 200 BCE–700 CE), after the Nasca culture developed out of the Paracas. In this period, a constellation of towns in the valleys and hills around the Nasca valley, including sites at La Quebrada del Frayle, Cahuachi, Palpa, and Ingenio, developed a sophisticated religious and artistic culture, noted for its weaving and pottery, and clever dry-land agricultural adaptations.

THE WORLD'S LARGEST ASTRONOMY BOOK

The discovery of the Nasca lines was attended by apparent mystery: here were magnificent and intricate artworks on a colossal scale, which must have required concerted planning and extreme effort, yet which can apparently only be seen from the air. How did their creators plan and execute such feats, by whom were they intended to be seen, and what was their purpose?

The notion that the lines can only be seen from the air is a fallacy easily debunked, although this has not prevented it from inspiring some fascinating fringe theories (see box on page 27). In fact, the glyphs on the hillsides were evidently made to be viewed from the plain, and the glyphs on the plain can be seen from the surrounding hills, although it may be that their true function depends on a much closer viewpoint (see below).

The first major theory about the function of the geoglyphs was archaeoastronomical (concerned with prehistoric astronomy), suggesting that, as with Stonehenge and many other classic earth mysteries, the Nasca lines relate to astronomy and the movement of the celestial bodies, particularly moments such as the equinoxes and solstices. This interpretation grew from an observation by the American archaeologist Paul Kosok, who was in South America studying ancient irrigation practices and became the first serious researcher into the Nasca lines. On the evening of June 22, 1941, the day after the winter solstice (Nasca being in the southern hemisphere), Kosok lifted his gaze from the line he was studying to find himself staring directly at the sunset, which was aligned with the line. Kosok posited astronomical alignments or representations for many of the major glyphs, describing the criss-crossed pampas as "the largest astronomy book in the world." He was succeeded in this school of interpretation by the German Maria Reiche.

Below: A bird's eye view of some of the lines and avenues; the wider figures might have provided ritual stages for gatherings.

THE RITUAL STAGE

Despite originally being the dominant interpretation, the archaeoastronomical explanation has largely fallen by the wayside. An early computer analysis of the lines, conducted by American astronomer Gerald Hawkins in 1968, found that the number of lines with astronomically significant alignments was no greater than would be found if they had been arranged purely at random. From the 1970s a new wave of researchers turned away from the picture of the lines' creators as ancient astronomical sages, and focused more on what would have been most important to the people who made them: water. For a society living on the edge of a desert and at the edge of sustainability, knowledge of rainfall patterns and water sources, and the rituals and beliefs around water and fertility, would have been primary.

The explorer and researcher Johan Reinhard suggests that "It seems likely that most of the lines did not point at anything on the geographical or celestial horizon, but rather led to places where rituals were performed to obtain water and fertility of crops." This interpretation is backed up by archaeological evidence. Some of the glyphs terminate at, surround, or radiate from ceremonial platforms, buried within which have been found offerings such as *Spondylus* shells, commonly associated in ancient Peruvian culture with water and fertility. Also found near the glyphs were seated human sacrifices—young men whose heads have been cut off and taken away, again a practice associated with rainfall and fertility rituals. One human sacrifice was accompanied by a jar showing a tree sprouting from a skull. Recent work on the glyphs has also emphasized the value of physically walking the lines in interpreting them. The act of walking them may have been part of a communal activity and performance tying together landscape, ritual, belief, and human relationships. The true purpose of the lines, then, may have been to function as a ceremonial stage for the participants and audience of rituals relating to water and fertility.

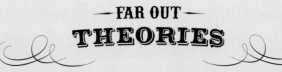

— FAR OUT —
THEORIES

Perhaps the most famous theory about the Nasca lines is that of Erich von Däniken, of "ancient astronaut" and *Chariots of the Gods?* fame. Von Däniken suggested that god-like beings featuring in ancient art and myths may have been extraterrestrial astronauts, and proposed that the Nasca geoglyphs look like airport runways because that is precisely what they were: landing strips for ancient astronauts—although the loose, uneven gravel of the pampas does not seem like the most practical surface on which to touch down your spaceship. Other theories predicated on the fallacy that the glyphs can only be truly appreciated from the sky include suggestions that they were made by and for shamans on drug- or trance-induced astral travels (out-of-body experiences where the consciousness is able to fly through the air and look around from an elevated perspective) and the ideas of explorer and aviator Jim Woodman. He described the lines as a "colossal puzzle," insisting that "You simply can't see anything

Above: Dubbed "The Astronaut," this anthropomorphic glyph has been seized upon by ancient astronaut theorists.

from ground level. You can't appreciate any of it from anywhere except from above." Dismissing the notion that the Nasca builders would have "gone to the monumental efforts they did without ever being able to see it," Woodman developed a theory that the Nasca possessed ancient hot-air balloon technology, and set about constructing a balloon using only materials that would have been available at the time. His balloon did manage to fly for a few minutes but his theory is widely dismissed as hot air.

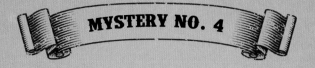
EASTER ISLAND

Date: *ca.* 1100–1700 CE
Location: Pacific Ocean

A remote Pacific Ocean island community, 2,300 miles (3,680 km) from Chile, is remarkable for its colossal stone busts, strange, indecipherable script, and puzzling societal collapse.

Easter Island is one of the planet's most remote pieces of land, yet when Dutch explorer Jacob Roggeveen came across it in 1722, he found it inhabited, and home to the remnants of an intriguing culture. The island has since emerged as one of the most mysterious places on Earth. It is most famous for its massive stone busts, known as moai, which stare broodingly from a landscape dramatically and catastrophically altered from what it once was. What is the moai's significance; how were they moved and erected; and why were most of them toppled? Alongside the moai are other mysteries: the indecipherable *rongorongo* script, perhaps encoding the lost language of Easter Island; the enigma of the collapse of Easter Island's civilization; the transformation of its ecosystem; and the riddle of the islanders' origins.

Today known to its indigenous inhabitants as Rapa Nui (although it is uncertain what they originally called it), Easter Island is located in the East Pacific, over 2,000 miles (3,200 km) from Tahiti in the west and 2,300 miles (3,680 km) from Chile to the east. It has an area of about 64 square miles (165 sq km) and rises to 16,870 feet (509 m) at its highest point. When Roggeveen arrived, he found a small population in reduced circumstances inhabiting a barren, treeless land, equipped with small canoes and with no domestic animals other than chickens. When Captain Cook visited the island 52 years later, he observed that almost all the colossal moai had been toppled. Over the next century the population was ravaged by introduced disease and the depredations of slave traders, until by the 1870s there were just 100 people living there, although the population has now recovered to over 3,000.

FLUSH WITH BUSTS

According to the most comprehensive survey yet undertaken of the busts, by archaeologist Jo Anne Van Tilburg, there are 887 moai on the island, carved from hardened volcanic ash known as tuff. The moai exist as part of a system; other elements include ahu,

Below: Easter Island moai, including a series arranged on an ahu (ceremonial platform), one of which bears a pukao (a cap that might represent hair).

or sacred platforms, on which the moai were intended to sit; and circular pukao—"caps" of a different type of lava (known as scoria), usually described as topknots, although they may be headdresses or stylized hair.

In the typical image of the moai, a huge head stares out to sea, but in reality only a minority of the busts ever made it to an ahu. Of the 887 moai, 397 (45 percent) still lie in the quarry at Rano Raraku where they were carved, 92 lie on roads leading out of the quarry, presumably having been abandoned in transit, and just 288 (32 percent) have been found at an ahu (the location of the remaining 110 being categorized as "other" in Van Tilburg's survey). The moai vary greatly in size; an average moai is 13 feet (4 m) high and weighs 14 tons (12.7 tonnes), but the largest is 72 feet (21.6 m) high and weighs around 187 tons (170 tonnes).

Jo Anne Van Tilburg believes the moai were created as representations of powerful chiefs, to act as mediators between earthly and supernatural realms. Many other interpretations

Left: A map showing where the majority of moai that made it out of the quarry were positioned around the coastline of the island.

Above: Like these examples, most of the moai never made it out of the Rano Raraku quarry.

are possible, however; for instance, did the statues originally stare out to sea (as those re-erected do today)? If so, might they have been guardians, protecting the island against malign external forces, or watchers, keeping a lookout for the return of mythical figures or messiahs?

Transporting and erecting the heavy statues must have been challenging for a society with relatively little technology. Rapa Nui folklore told of the statues walking to their sites, or of special individuals gifted with powerful mana (spiritual energy) moving them by magic. Most theories posit the use of wooden sledges or rollers, with ropes and A-frame-type crane-scaffolds. Moist organic matter, such as banana skins or sweet potatoes, might have helped lubricate the process. Pits and ramps could also have helped raise and lower the moai into position, and to place the pukao on top.

COLLAPSE AND CANNIBALISM

The mystery of moai transportation may be linked to the riddle of the collapse of Easter Island society. Analysis of pollen and archaeological remains shows that the island once supported a much richer ecosystem. It was forested, and inhabitants used sophisticated intensive farming techniques, such as lithic mulches (growing crops between stones to protect the soil from erosion and slow evaporation) and irrigation to grow taro. They built large canoes, enabling them to hunt dolphin, porpoise, and tuna, supplementing the seabirds, fish, and shellfish they could catch along the coast.

The era of moai building may have begun as early as 1100 CE (although some sources claim that the island was not settled until *ca*. 1200), and the last moai was probably erected around 1620. From the late 16th century, the archaeological record reveals, the island was afflicted by a worsening ecological catastrophe, with deforestation leading to soil erosion and loss of fertility, and the collapse of agricultural productivity. At the same time, lack of timber made it impossible to build large ocean-going boats, limiting the potential to hunt. Having reached a peak of perhaps over 10,000 people in around 1550, the population plunged as starvation, civil strife, and even cannibalism took hold.

The old social system collapsed, symbolized by the toppling of most of the island's moai around 1680. What led to the deforestation? An obvious potential culprit is the excessive use of timber for moai construction and transport. It may simply be, however, that the population had expanded beyond the carrying capacity of the island's fragile ecosystem.

RONGORONGO TEXTS

The society's collapse, followed by the destruction of most of the surviving population, left behind another mystery: the meaning of a mysterious script engraved on artifacts such as wooden tablets, and known as *rongorongo*. One theory is that *rongorongo* was only invented in the 18th century after contact with Spanish writing prompted the islanders to develop their own script, but some inscriptions seem to date to the 17th century, suggesting an earlier, possibly indigenous origin. The script seems to mix ideographs (picture writing where each symbol equates to a word or concept) with symbols representing syllables or sounds, but the paucity of surviving texts means it is impossible to reconstruct for certain. This has not prevented multiple efforts; Steven Fischer, who also claims to have deciphered the Phaistos Disk, has compared *rongorongo* to writing on a South American staff and used this to decipher *rongorongo* inscriptions as creation chants.

— FAR OUT —
THEORIES

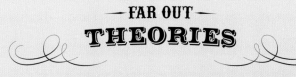

The Easter Island heads have become almost synonymous with the ancient astronaut school of mysteries. In his 1970 book *Return to the Stars*, Erich von Däniken claims "A small group of intelligent beings [i.e. aliens] was stranded on Easter Island owing to a 'technical hitch' . . . they made . . . stone giants which they set up on stone pedestals along the coast so that they were visible from afar." The distinctive appearance of the moai is seen as a clue to the appearance of extraterrestrials, although in fact they closely resemble statues from other Polynesian islands.

The origin of the Easter Islanders has also attracted exotic hypotheses, most famously the contention of Norwegian explorer and anthropologist Thor Heyerdahl that they were settled from South America, not Polynesia as is conventionally assumed. This would explain how the Easter Islanders came to possess the sweet potato—originally from South America—and also account for the striking similarity between the

Above: A close-up view shows the technical proficiency of mortarless masonry at an Easter Island ahu.

mortarless drystone walls of the Inca, and some of the drystone walls on Easter Island, which attracted the attention of Captain Cook in 1774. He later wrote: "The workmanship is not inferior to the best plain piece of masonry we have in England. They use no sort of cement; yet the joints are exceedingly close, and the stones morticed and tenanted [sic] one into another." Linguistic, cultural, archaeological, anatomical, and genetic evidence, however, all points to a Polynesian origin for Easter Islanders.

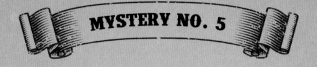

ROSSLYN CHAPEL

Date: 1446
Location: Roslin, near Edinburgh, Scotland

The unique, ornate medieval chapel featured in Dan Brown's *The Da Vinci Code* has been linked to the Knights Templar, the Holy Grail, and the pre-Columbian exploration of America.

Rosslyn Chapel, officially named the Collegiate Church of St. Matthew the Apostle, is situated in Roslin in southern Scotland, just south of Edinburgh. It was founded in 1446 by Sir William St. Clair, a Scottish knight of Norman descent, who was one of the most powerful barons in Scotland and had many illustrious ancestors and descendants. The colorful history of the St. Clair (aka Sinclair) family, particularly their associations with crusading and later with the Freemasons, coupled with the extraordinary richness and symbolism of the carvings in the chapel, have proved to be fertile soil for the imaginations of "alternative historians."

Sir William St. Clair intended to build a much larger structure than the surviving chapel, but he never got further than building the choir. Construction was halted on his death, and a roof was

Above: An interior view of Rosslyn Chapel, showing the ornate Prentice Pillar next to the seated figure in the background.

put over the choir, thus forming the chapel. Fourteen pillars hold up the roof and there is a lower church or crypt. Below this there are vaults in which the St. Clairs were buried for many generations, although these are now filled in with fine, sandy soil. The whole interior is covered with an exuberant proliferation of carving, including many natural and vegetative forms, faces, grotesques, blocks, and abstract patterns. Particularly famous are two of the pillars: a mildly ornate one known as the Master Pillar, and an extremely ornate one known as the Prentice (or Apprentice) Pillar.

The popular legend is that the Prentice Pillar was started by a master mason who decided to visit Rome for inspiration before he completed it, only to discover on his return that his apprentice had not only finished the job for him (after receiving inspiration in a dream), but had put him to shame with the quality of his craft. In a fit of jealous rage, the master killed the apprentice with a hammer blow to the head. Supposedly, one of the carved heads in the chapel represents the murdered apprentice, complete with a scar on his head. In fact, the names for the pillars only date to the 18th century, and the tale of the murdered apprentice is common to many sites and probably reflects a popular Masonic legend. Other intriguing carvings include several Green Men, figures with pagan associations appropriated by Christianity; minstrels playing instruments; skeletons; foliage, fruits, flowers, and crops; and grinning faces and masks.

THE ST. CLAIRS OF ROSSLYN

Father Richard Augustine Hay's *1700 Genealogie of the Saintclaires of Rosslyn* records that "It came into [William St. Clair's] mind to build a house for God's service, of most curious work." The St. Clair family, which still owns the chapel today, is descended from the Norman St. Clairs who came over with William the Conqueror. Sir Henry St. Clair, the 2nd Baron of Rosslyn, went on the First Crusade, while the 7th Baron, also Sir Henry, fought with Robert the Bruce at Bannockburn, and his son William was one of the knights tasked with bearing the late king's heart to Jerusalem for burial, although he was killed en route in a battle with the Moors in Spain in 1330. The 9th Baron became the Prince of Orkney in 1379, and his grandson William, the 11th Baron of Rosslyn and 3rd Prince of Orkney, founded the chapel. On his death in 1484 he was buried in the vaults, but his son failed to continue with construction, perhaps because of the massive cost of the project. The ornate carvings of the chapel were lucky to survive the Reformation, and during the

Opposite: This stone angel at Rosslyn Chapel bears a shield with what might be a Templar cross. The emblem was probably added in the 19th century.

Below: A Green Man carving in the chapel. Although they may have their roots in paganism, Green Men came to be Christian symbols common in churches.

Civil War Oliver Cromwell ordered all of the altars to be smashed. The chapel was abandoned and fell into ruin until 1736; this same year the St. Clairs, who had long held the hereditary position of Grand Master Mason of Scotland from the stonemasons' guild, began their long association with Freemasonry, when the 19th Baron was elected Grand Master by the new Scottish Lodges of Freemasonry.

SECRETS OF THE CHAPEL

The chapel attracted the attention of writers and artists such as Robert Burns, Walter Scott, and William Wordsworth. Scott made the chapel a central player in a novel about the Knights Templar, and in the late 18th and early 19th centuries many Masonic lodges liked to play up their supposed descent from groups such as the Templars. But it was not until the 1980s that the chapel began in earnest its other life as a place of mystery, conspiracy, and alternative history. In 1982 Michael Baigent, Richard Leigh, and Henry Lincoln published *The Holy Blood and The Holy Grail*, a bestselling book that practically founded an entire genre of publishing: alternative or pseudo-history. In their book Baigent, Leigh, and Lincoln laid out an extraordinary tale of conspiracy, cover-up, and lost history.

The role of Rosslyn Chapel in this elaborate drama was more fully explored in the 1988 book *The Temple and The Lodge* by Michael Baigent and Richard Leigh, and in 2003 the author Dan Brown used these earlier books as inspiration for the global phenomenon *The Da Vinci Code*, made into a film in 2006. The supposed truth on which the *Code* is based is that the St. Clairs were Templar stalwarts, and that when the order was suppressed in 1312 it survived in Scotland. Accordingly, its precious secrets, including relics of unimaginable sanctity, were passed to the St. Clairs for safe keeping, and William St. Clair built Rosslyn Chapel to store and safeguard them, and also to encode their secrets in the elaborate carvings. The relics that lie hidden in the chapel, possibly in the vaults or even within the Prentice Pillar, might include the Holy Grail itself (although the point of the original *Holy Blood* book was that the true nature of the Grail was the actual bloodline of Christ), or some other sacred artifacts—perhaps the True Cross, the Ark of the Covenant, or lost gospels; all have been suggested.

TEMPLAR TRIPE

In fact, there is an historical basis for imagining secrets hidden in the chapel. In 1546, Mary of Guise, wife of James V and mother of Mary Queen of Scots, wrote to Sir William St. Clair, grandson of the chapel's founder: "Likewise that we shall be Leal and trew Maistres to him, his Counsill and Secret shewn to us we sall keep secret." But almost every other piece of evidence adduced in favor of the Holy Grail theory falls apart under scrutiny. The St. Clairs, for instance, were never Templars; in fact, when the Templars were brought to trial in Edinburgh for heresy and impropriety in 1309, the St. Clairs of Rosslyn testified against them. Freemasonry has no genuine links to the Templars. *The Holy Blood and the Holy Grail*'s story proved to be based on the fantasies of a convicted French con man with links to the far right, who had smuggled forged documents into the Bibliotheque Nationale to back up his preposterous tale (see "Rennes-le-Château," page 56). Masonic imagery in Rosslyn Chapel was added in the 1860s by the Fourth Earl of Rosslyn, an ardent Mason who was replacing severely corroded carvings. The vaults beneath the chapel cannot be excavated without undermining the building, but are believed to contain only the graves of St. Clairs. It has been claimed that

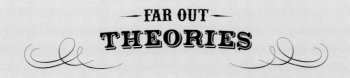

— FAR OUT —
THEORIES

In their 1982 book *The Holy Blood and The Holy Grail*, Michael Baigent, Richard Leigh, and Henry Lincoln claimed to have found documentary evidence showing that a super-secret society had been engaged for millennia in a battle with the forces of the Catholic Church to protect the true legacy of Jesus—his bloodline, in the shape of descendants of his relationship with Mary Magdalene. Supposedly, Jesus had survived or dodged the Crucifixion, and he, Mary, and their children had been spirited off to southern France, where their descendants had gone on to found the Merovingian dynasty of Frankish kings. According to the theory, the mainstream Catholic Church, in league with various state powers from the Carolingians to the European

Above: A tomb in Rosslyn Chapel said to be that of a Templar knight, although in practice the St. Clairs were no friends of the order.

Union, had spent thousands of years trying to suppress this secret history, but a secret society sworn to protect the holy bloodline had set up front groups, including the Templars, the Rosicrucians, and the Freemasons, to keep the flame alive.

medieval carvings of corn (maize) and aloe in the chapel show that the St. Clairs used the Templar fleet to cross the Atlantic centuries before Columbus. In fact, these carvings do not show maize and aloe, but are supposed to be either stylized wood or arum lilies. The Templars did not have a fleet of their own, and certainly did not possess ocean-going ships.

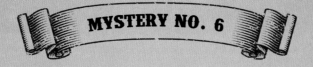

EL DORADO

Date: 1538
Location: Somewhere in South America

The search for El Dorado, South America's legendary lost city of gold, is a twisted and ultimately futile tale of greed, insanity, and tragedy, played out over centuries and across a continent.

The Spanish conquistadors who ravaged the great Aztec and Inca civilizations became fabulously wealthy, but they always lusted after more. In South America, Francisco Pizarro and his men captured the Inca emperor Atahualpa, who boggled their minds by offering a ransom of enough gold and silver to fill a room. After they betrayed and murdered him, his successor Manco Inca took up resistance to the Spanish, retreating with the remaining Inca forces to wage a guerrilla campaign from secret forts in the jungles and mountains. The conquistadors believed that Manco had spirited away the true wealth of the Inca Empire—suspicions that were inflamed by popular legends in which defiant natives gathered together huge piles of corn, before presenting the Spanish with a single kernel. This kernel, said the natives, represented the proportion of the Inca treasure the Spanish had managed to get their hands on—the rest would never be theirs.

TALES FROM THE INTERIOR

The story of El Dorado really begins in 1538, when a native carrying messages for the deceased Inca emperor was captured by the Spanish at Cajamarca. He had come from the interior, and when questioned he revealed an intriguing story. To the east of his homeland, he said, was a tribe who practiced an annual ceremony to appease their gods. Their king was stripped naked and covered in balsam gum, whereupon priests would blow gold dust at him until he was coated with a layer of the precious substance. Embarking on a great raft, surrounded by priests and nobles, the king would be rowed out into the center of a sacred lake, before he dived into the water to wash himself clean. Meanwhile, offerings of gold and other treasures were thrown into the lake. On hearing this tale, the conquistador captain Sebastián de Benalcázar dubbed this gold-coated monarch El Dorado—the gilded one.

Below: John Everett Millais's *Pizarro Seizing the Inca of Peru* depicts the capture of Atahualpa by the conquistadors.

The story was probably based on truth—an account of the practices of a neighboring tribe called the Muisca. They lived in the highlands of present-day Colombia and their worship had been based around Lake Guatavitá, a sacred lake in the hills high above modern-day Bogotá. The Muisca had long before been conquered by a neighboring tribe, so if the tale had ever been true the ritual was no longer practiced. But who knew how many years of loot might be piled up at the bottom of the lake?

THE SACRED LAKE

Benalcázar launched the first of many expeditions seeking the golden king and his city of gold. Brutally difficult exploration brought him, in 1539, to the territories of the Muisca, only to discover that another conquistador captain, Gonzalo Jiménez de Quesada, had already got there in 1537, establishing the colony of Bogotá. While the Muisca had enough gold to whet his appetite, de Quesada was disappointed to learn that they had no gold mines. He did, however, through bullying and torture, learn the location of the sacred Lake Guatavitá.

In 1562, the merchant and engineer Antonio de Sepúlveda launched a determined effort to search the lake for gold. He cut a deep notch in the rim of the crater surrounding the lake and drained the water via a ditch. The level was reduced by around 60 feet (20 m) before a collapse killed many of the workers. De Sepúlveda recovered artifacts including a staff covered in gold and an emerald the size of an egg, but a muddy lake bottom was hardly the city of gold the conquistadors still believed lay somewhere in the jungle and mountains.

OMAGUA AND THE AMAZON

In 1541, a German expedition explored new parts of the Andes and brought back legends of a city called Omagua, said to be overflowing with gold and emeralds. That same year, Francisco Pizarro dispatched his brother Gonzalo on an entrada to cross the Andes and penetrate the rainforest on the other side. The younger Pizarro became separated from his partner, Francisco de Orellana, and endured a nightmare of disease, starvation, hostile natives, and implacable wilderness. De Orellana, meanwhile, built boats to travel down the Amazon River (named for de Orellana's account of a tribe of fierce warrior women) but he was to become severely ill and die in his attempt to find Omagua and El Dorado. An even more brutal fate was to befall the young soldier Pedro de Ursúa in 1560. The new Viceroy of Peru had decided to launch an expedition to occupy restive conquistadors, led by de Ursúa, who had a beautiful female companion. Jealousy about the alluring woman and extreme hardships in the wilderness fomented discord, and on New Year's Day 1561 mutineers stabbed de Ursúa to death.

A veteran soldier from Europe, Don Antonio de Berrio, arrived in Bogotá in 1580 to take up an inheritance from his wife's uncle, Gonzalo Jiménez de Quesada himself. It stipulated he must pursue the search for El Dorado. De Berrio was already 60 years old, but he too would spend many more years in fruitless pursuit of a mirage.

Below: The sacred Lake Guatavitá—a volcanic lagoon, lying 10,000 feet (3,300 m) above sea level.

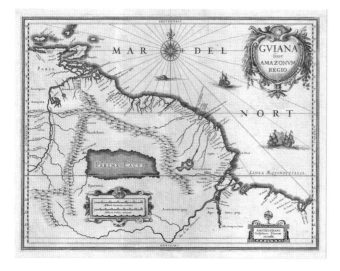

Above: Dutch cartographer Willem Blaeu's 1635 map of the northeast of South America, largely based on Walter Raleigh's accounts—featuring Lake Paríma and the road to El Dorado.

RALEIGH'S DISCOVERY

After decades of failed attempts, a new entrant joined the crowded field: Sir Walter Raleigh. He arrived in the New World in 1595 with a squadron of ships and captured Trinidad—an island off the mouth of the Orinoco River, where de Berrio was by then based— as well as de Berrio himself. Exploring the Orinoco River, Raleigh found evidence of gold mines and learned stories, already familiar to de Berrio, of a rich Inca city called Manoa, built on a lake called Paríma. Returning to England, Raleigh wrote a book called *The Discoverie*, introducing the legend of El Dorado to the European mainstream, with maps showing Paríma and Manoa, which would become the standard guide for explorers for centuries.

In England Raleigh fell foul of the new monarch, James I, and was locked in the Tower. Back in Guyana, de Berrio was competing with Raleigh's lieutenant Keylis to find Manoa. The search was fruitless: each tribe they encountered would direct them further on. In 1597, financially, physically, and spiritually exhausted, de Berrio passed away with the bitter epitaph, "If you try to do too much you will end by doing nothing at all."

THE END OF THE AFFAIR

In 1616 Raleigh finally secured his release and returned to the New World; only death and misery awaited him. His son was killed in a skirmish with the Spanish, leading to a falling out with Keylis, who committed suicide. On his return to England he was seized and convicted of fomenting war with the Spanish, and

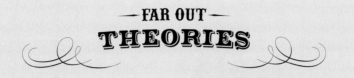

— FAR OUT —
THEORIES

The appetites of the treasure hunters were further whetted by the story of Juan Martinez, a Spaniard who emerged from the jungle in 1586 claiming to be the sole survivor of an expedition attacked by natives. He said that he had been led to a great city called Manoa, where he had met El Dorado, the gilded one, in person. Eventually he was allowed to return to his people, laden with treasures, and although he had lost most of these on the way back he apparently possessed enough to lend credibility to his tale.

Above: The fabulous wealth looted from indigenous peoples simply stoked the greed of the conquistadors.

executed in 1618. Raleigh's maps continued to inspire fruitless searching, and it was not until 1800, when the Guyanese uplands were properly charted by professional explorers like Alexander von Humboldt, that Lake Paríma and Manoa were proven to be imaginary. Attention turned back to Lake Guatavitá, fanned by speculations on the quantity of treasure that might lurk at the bottom—up to a billion pounds sterling (around $120 billion today), according to an 1825 travel guide. In 1912 a mechanized attempt was made to drain the lake, but the muddy floor dried solid before it could be dredged and the expedition ended in failure. In recent times, the lake has been a protected zone, and the treasure of El Dorado must remain legendary and lost.

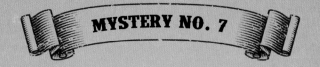

THE OAK ISLAND MONEY PIT

Date: 1795
Location: Oak Island, Nova Scotia, Canada

For over a century, treasure hunters have sought to gain entry to a Canadian island pit, in pursuit of hidden loot variously linked to everyone from the Knights Templar to William Shakespeare. But each time they draw close, a disaster occurs.

The Oak Island story has become a well-worn folk yarn, but the oldest sources of the tale are newspaper accounts from the mid-19th century, which relate events said to have begun much earlier. In 1795 young Daniel McGinnis (or McInnis, or McInnies) was exploring the half-square-mile island, possibly drawn there by reports of strange lights. While roaming, he came upon a suspicious-looking shallow depression in the ground beneath an overhanging branch—in some versions, the telltale detail is an old pulley hanging directly above the hollow.

His curiosity aroused, McGinnis recruited two friends to help him dig, and found a pit filled with loose soil. A little below the surface the men found a layer of flagstones, and beyond that, a layer of beams or logs. They were now convinced this was a man-made pit. The coast abounded with rumors of hidden pirate gold,

particularly in connection to the notorious Captain Kidd; could McGinnis have stumbled upon the long-dead brigand's main stash?

The three men returned with help a few years later and began a full excavation. As they dug deeper, they encountered successive layers—more platforms of oak logs or beams, layers of clay and charcoal, and matting similar to coconut fiber. In some versions, strange markings were found in the shaft. But when the dig reached a climax, with the apparent discovery of a chest, the shaft suddenly flooded and could not be drained.

FORTY FEET BELOW

A series of increasingly involved excavations followed, featuring heavy machinery and mining gear. The legend of the Money Pit attracted investors and adventurers, including such luminaries as Franklin D. Roosevelt (who actually spent some time on the island helping with the excavations) and John Wayne. Exploratory

Above: Works at a dig site on Oak Island, photographed in the 1930s; the island has been the scene of excavations for over a hundred years.

drilling brought up a core of material that supposedly included links from a gold chain. Some accounts speak of old tools and fragments of parchment, while a stone tablet inscribed with a coded message was allegedly found in the early 19th century, only to disappear and then reappear in 1919. The only evidence of the stone is a 1970 "record" of the markings, which were decoded and apparently spelled out the message: "Forty Feet Below Two Million Pounds Are Buried." A video camera lowered down a borehole in 1971 obtained indistinct footage, which was said to show a wooden chest and a severed hand.

But every excavation ended similarly. Just as a promising level or chamber was reached, the shaft would collapse or the bottom would give way and water would rush in and flood the pit. This even happened to the many parallel shafts that were bored. The work also proved dangerous: in the 19th century, one man died when a boiler blew up and another when a hoist broke, while in 1965 four miners were asphyxiated by gas.

Opposite: The notorious 17th-century pirate Captain Kidd. Does Oak Island conceal a hoard of his buried loot?

Below: Future president Franklin D. Roosevelt (center, with pipe) and chums, pictured on Oak Island in 1910.

The failure of even the most professional attempts has led to speculation about the seemingly impressive engineering skills of the pit's constructors. Somehow, using pre-19th-century technology, they had dug a shaft over 100 feet (30 m) deep, and rigged it to include a series of elaborate water traps, where any "unauthorized" breach of the main treasure chamber would result in its collapse.

MYSTERY ENGINEERS

Two centuries of excavations on Oak Island have taken their toll. The island is riddled with so many parallel and subsidiary shafts and boreholes that the location of the original pit has been lost, while any information that a serious archaeological survey might have gleaned has been hopelessly contaminated by the dozens of digs. Treasure hunters, however, are undaunted, and further explorations are planned for the future. What might they find, and is there really anything there to discover?

Since the story of the Money Pit first surfaced, speculation has been rife. In addition to the legendary loot of Captain Kidd, a variety of other pirates were proposed as the pit's originators, including Blackbeard (Edward Teach) and Henry Morgan. Other theories included Spanish survivors of a treasure galleon blown off course, or British sailors who had captured such a galleon and did not want to pay tax on their haul. Lending credence to these suggestions was the fact that both pirates and the British Navy had been known to frequent Mahone Bay, where Oak Island is located. Also, the apparent structure of the pit was said to resemble British military engineering techniques used in the 17th century.

But perhaps no one is responsible for digging the Money Pit. A survey of Oak Island by the Woods Hole Oceanographic Institute in 1995 concluded that the pit was most likely the result of natural processes. The geology of the island lends itself to the formation of underground caverns, and these sometimes collapse, causing a sinkhole or pit to open up. These pits may then be filled in with soil and other debris over time, with layers of fallen logs and branches washed in during floods or storms. The end result could appear to an excavator like an artificially constructed and filled in pit. The constant flooding of the excavated shaft can be explained by the presence of fissures and cracks that allow seawater to penetrate deep into the island.

THE POE CONNECTION

If the pit is just a natural feature, how did it acquire such a body of legend? There are no accounts of the Money Pit contemporary with the date of its alleged discovery: the earliest come from newspaper reports of the 1850s and '60s, a period when papers were well known for inventing stories and even running "tall tale telling" competitions. The Money Pit yarn has all the ingredients of such a tale, and it may not be a coincidence that it resembles the popular Edgar Allen Poe short story *The Gold Bug*, which had come out a few years earlier (in 1843). Poe's tale concerns a buried treasure—possibly Captain Kidd's—discovered when a rope dangling from an overhanging branch reveals the location of a pit.

Subsequent details of the legend, such as the gold links and old tools recovered by excavators, or the cipher stone pulled from the pit, are equally suspect. The former may simply be inventions, or if real they could have been "salted" by prospectors looking to drum up investment. As for the stone, there is no proof that it ever existed, and the "transcription" from 1970 is almost certainly an invention. So the Money Pit may be nothing more than an out-of-control newspaper prank, which accumulated spurious details as its legend grew, and cost money and lives that were all too real.

— FAR OUT —
THEORIES

Above: William Shakespeare: not the author of his works, according to a theory that links the pit to Francis Bacon.

Although originally associated with legends of pirate gold, today the pit is most commonly linked to the Knights Templar. It is seen as the final destination for riches smuggled out of France and taken to Scotland under the protection of the St. Clair family (see page 34). The family's Norse heritage (via the Normans) supposedly gave them access to the secrets of transatlantic travel before Columbus, allowing Henry St. Clair to navigate the Templar fleet to Nova Scotia, arriving on Oak Island where the Templars employed the secrets of monumental masonry (handed down to them from dwellers of ancient Atlantis (see page 10) via the Temple builders, and later passed on to the Freemasons) to construct the Money Pit. The upshot of this fantastic tale is that the Money Pit might conceal anything from stacks of Templar bullion to the Holy Grail itself. But this theory should also be seen in the light of the racist agenda that attempts to prove pre-Columbian title to the Americas for whites. Other outlandish candidates for creators of the Money Pit include space aliens, Incas or Aztecs hiding gold from the conquistadors, and the true author of Shakespeare's works. Dr. Orville Ward Owen claimed to have decoded ciphers that prove the leading Elizabethan philosopher and statesman Sir Francis Bacon was the true author of Shakespeare's plays, and that he had hidden documents proving this in the Money Pit.

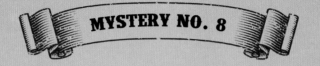

THE WINCHESTER MYSTERY HOUSE

Date: 1884–1922
Location: San Jose, California, USA

The curious Winchester Mystery House is now a major tourist attraction, but during its thirty-eight-year construction this wealthy heiress's home was possibly something much stranger: a decades-long negotiation with spirits of the dead.

Sarah Winchester, née Pardee, was the wife of William Wirt Winchester, heir to the Winchester Rifle fortune. When her father-in-law Oliver Fisher Winchester, manufacturer of the Winchester repeating rifle, died in 1880, followed four months later by his son William, Sarah Winchester was left a very rich widow. By this time, however, she was a tragic figure, plunged into depression by the death in 1866 of her infant daughter, Annie.

Seeking answers or comfort, Sarah Winchester did the same as many in this era: she turned to a medium, a person who claimed to be able to communicate with the spirits of the dead. Exactly what Mrs. Winchester was told or came to believe is the subject of speculation, since she never gave an interview, left a diary, or in any other way recorded her thoughts and motivations. According to legend, however, she was told that her tragic ill luck was due

Left: A front view of
the Winchester Mystery
House in San Jose,
California.

to the unwholesome attentions of the vengeful spirits of those
soldiers, cowboys, and Indians shot down by her father-in-law's
rifles, which had first become popular with the Union army in
the Civil War, and the subsequent Winchester 1873 had become
known as the "Gun that Won the West." Furthermore, the story
goes, the medium told Mrs. Winchester that, in order to either
evade or appease the spirits, she should move out West and build
a house. Not just any house, though: one that would either shelter
or confuse the spirits, depending on the version of the tale. In
particular, the widow was supposedly told, the house must never
be finished. So long as it were under construction, Mrs. Winchester
would be spared the further depredations of the spirit world.
Whether this injunction was ever uttered is unclear; it seems more
likely that this is a post-hoc rationalization for what came after.

WAY OUT WEST

Whether or not dispatched by supernatural exhortation, Mrs.
Winchester did indeed move West. Visiting her niece in California,
she found a suitable spot in the Santa Clara Valley, just a few miles

from San Jose, and in 1884 she bought a farm there and started building, using an existing eight-room farmhouse as a starting point. Over the next four decades Mrs. Winchester kept the house under continuous construction, hiring shifts of workmen to build round the clock. By 1900 the humble farmhouse had metastasized into a seven-story mansion, and by the time she died in 1922 the building sprawled across six acres and had 160 rooms, along with 6 kitchens, 13 bathrooms, 47 stairways and fireplaces, 2,000 doors, and 10,000 windows.

But the house was not simply large. Mrs. Winchester was unconstrained by building controls or budget (the death of her mother-in-law in 1897 meant that her share in the Winchester Repeating Arms Company brought her a staggering income of $1,000—equivalent to around $30,000 in modern money—per day!), and she issued new instructions every day. Rooms were constantly remodeled or simply demolished and replaced, and this led to many bizarre developments: staircases and doorways that led nowhere, windows overlooking other rooms, chimneys that did not reach the ceiling. An estimated 500–600 rooms were built in total, but only 160 remain, and even these proved hard to count because the layout of the house is so confusing. Mrs. Winchester had a fixation with the number 13. For instance, among many other instances, she had 13 panes in many windows and 13 steps on many staircases, 13 ceiling panels in some rooms, and 13 holes in the drain covers in the sinks.

No architect drew up a masterplan for the convoluted and contorted monster that resulted; according to legend, the instructions were issued by the spirits, or at least divined by Mrs. Winchester during nightly briefings. In the center of the house was the Blue Room, where Mrs. Winchester would hold a séance every night, wearing one of 13 special colored robes that hung from 13 hooks. Supposedly a bell could be heard ringing at midnight and 2am each night, to mark the hours of

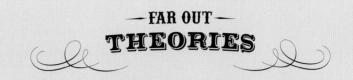

— FAR OUT — THEORIES

Above: The Door to Nowhere, one of the Mystery House's characteristic oddities.

There was said to be something spooky about the widow Mrs. Winchester herself, since she availed herself of secret passages and hidden doors to spy and creep up on her servants. In 1928, *The American Weekly* magazine imagined her nightly progress: "When Mrs. Winchester set out for her Séance Room, it might well have discouraged the ghost of the Indian or even of a bloodhound, to follow her. After traversing an interminable labyrinth of rooms and hallways, suddenly she would push a button, a panel would fly back and she would step quickly from one apartment into another, and unless the pursuing ghost was watchful and quick, he would lose her . . . This was supposed to be very discomforting to evil spirits who are said to be naturally suspicious of traps."

arrival and departure of the spirits. But was she helping or hiding from the ghosts? Apparently Mrs. Winchester slept in a different bedroom each night to avoid the spirits, and the constantly changing floorplan was devised to throw them off her trail, but at the same time she allowed only a couple of mirrors in the house because spirits must not see their own reflections, and she installed many brilliant lights because spirits were said (somewhat counter-intuitively) to dislike shadows.

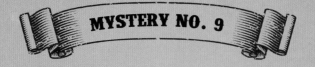

RENNES-LE-CHÂTEAU

Date: 1896
Location: Languedoc, France

The village of Rennes-le-Château lies in the heartland of the Cathars, a heretical Christian sect suppressed long ago but linked to tales of treasure both monetary and occult—rumors of which bring thousands of tourists a year.

The reason for the extraordinary popularity of Rennes-le-Château is the legend of Bérenger Saunière. Saunière was a lowly priest appointed to the poor backwater parish of Rennes, in the foothills of the Pyrenees, in 1885. In 1896 he began to spend lavishly, and in very peculiar ways. He paid for expensive renovations and redecorations of the parish church, including the installation of Stations of the Cross featuring incongruous elements such as a boy wearing a kilt; an inscription above the entrance that read, *"Terribilis locus iste"* ("This is a terrible place"); and a grotesque statue of a devil, crouching in the porch.

Saunière also bought up tracts of land around the village, building an imposing house, the Villa Bethania, and a library housed in a folly known as the Magdala Tower. He spent lavishly on hobbies such as stamp- and book-collecting, gathered a menagerie of exotic animals, and hosted decadent parties. He traveled to Paris and gained entrée to the salons of the demi-monde, mingling with people of influence and figures from the occult world. The Church disapproved of his profligate spending and Saunière was suspended from his duties. However, he refused to leave the village, and was still making grand plans when he died in 1917.

THE LEGEND OF BÉRENGER SAUNIÈRE

The mystery of Saunière's sudden wealth lingered unsolved until the 1950s, when a story began to circulate. It was said that the abbé had stumbled upon mysterious documents hidden within a "Visigothic" pillar in the church (Rennes had been an important site during the Visigothic era of the 6th and 7th centuries CE)— tourists can see the pillar today, in the village's Saunière Museum. The hidden parchments were written in Latin, and in code.

Below: The lurid devil that guards the entrance to the parish church of Rennes.

In 1969, British writer Henry Lincoln investigated these mysterious parchments, presenting documentaries on the subject, and later co-writing *The Holy Blood and the Holy Grail*, the book that inspired *The Da Vinci Code* (see page 39). These books claimed the parchments revealed Christ's descendants had come to France and ruled as the Merovingian dynasty, but had later been suppressed by the Catholic Church. To protect the holy bloodline, a secretive but immensely influential society, the Priory of Sion, had been set up. Counting luminaries from da Vinci to Isaac Newton to Voltaire among its Grand Masters, the Priory had also operated via the Cathars and the Templars—both in on the explosive secret—and later through Masonic groups to contend with the Church for hegemony of Europe. Lincoln claimed Saunière had stumbled upon this web of secrets, and had bartered them into power and popularity. Possibly he had also recovered hidden Cathar or Templar gold, stashed under or near Rennes.

Above: The "Visigothic" pillar in which Saunière allegedly discovered secret documents; it is probably bogus.

HOUSE OF CARDS

The Da Vinci Code claims to be based on historical fact. The story of Saunière and his parchments are central to this mythos, but they make shaky foundations for a house of cards. Saunière was undoubtedly eccentric, made strange alterations to his adopted village, and kept eclectic company. But there is no evidence that he found any scrolls or dug up any treasures. The purported "Visigoth" pillar is probably a fake and there is no evidence it was ever in the church in Rennes. His "inexplicable" wealth has probably been wildly overstated, and toward the end of his life he was so poor he was reduced to asking for loans.

The true source of his money was almost certainly the illegal practice of selling masses—which is why he was suspended by the Church. The strange decorations he added to the church at Rennes probably relate to his political views, which were radically pro-Royalist and in favor of recombining Church and State, and the symbolism of the devil and other changes reflect this. Even the peculiar inscription over the entrance to the church might have an innocuous explanation—it could be a reference to a mass said when dedicating a church, with *"terribilis"* read in the sense of "awesome" rather than "terrible." Despite the reams of text written on the matter, no treasure or relics have ever been discovered in or around Rennes.

THE GREAT RENNES HOAX

If Saunière was simply a corrupt priest, where did these extraordinary legends spring from? Most of them can be traced back to hoaxes and fraudsters. The first of these was Noël Corbu, the new owner of an eatery in the Villa Bethania—Saunière's old

Below: The tomb of Bérenger Saunière. But was he the keeper of ancient secrets or a corrupt clergyman?

home—who hoped to drum up custom by peddling a juicy treasure mystery. In 1956, French newspapers caught on to Corbu's yarn and the hoax began to snowball. Rennes became established as a focus for mystery seekers and treasure hunters.

From here the hoax was taken on by the unsavory fraudster Pierre Plantard. Plantard held reactionary pro-Royalist, anti-Semitic views and developed an elaborate fantasy in which he became a key figure in French history. Plantard claimed to be the last scion of a royal house that traced its antecedents back to the Merovingian kings, and which awaited its chance to regain the throne, institute a sort of neo-fascist utopia, and restore France to greatness (see also "Rosslyn Chapel," page 34). Included in this fiction was the shadowy Priory of Sion, supposedly founded a thousand years ago. Documents in the French national archives at the Bibliothèque Nationale appeared to support this tale, but in fact these were forgeries planted by Plantard's cronies. The Priory did exist, but only because it had been founded in 1956 by Plantard himself as a vehicle for his religious-nationalist preoccupations.

JOINING THE DOTS

Plantard co-produced *The Gold of Rennes* (1967; later even more dramatically retitled *The Cursed Treasure of Rennes-le-Château*), a book placing Rennes at the center of the fantasy. Included were alleged copies of the actual documents Saunière had recovered from his hollow pillar, complete with coded references to the Priory. The book was a bestseller, but Plantard's fiction really went global with the tremendous success of 1982's *Holy Blood*, which expanded the story to connect Rennes and the Priory to the Holy Grail and the bloodline of Christ, including the startling revelation that Plantard was a descendant of Jesus and Mary Magdalene.

This house of cards could not stand up to scrutiny, and it was soon demolished by researchers, and by confessions by many of those involved in the hoax. Plantard was exposed as a con artist and

— FAR OUT — THEORIES

Since the publication of *The Holy Blood and the Holy Grail* and *The Da Vinci Code*, multiple books have claimed that Rennes and the surrounding area are home to everything from the tomb of Christ and Mary Magdalene to the Ark of the Covenant and the Holy Grail. It has been suggested that the hills and valleys of the region have been chosen or even shaped—using ancient lore dating back to the Temple builders, the Egyptians, and even the Atlanteans, of the ancient island empire of Atlantis (see page 10)—into a sacred landscape, with meaning and symbolism carved into every contour.

Above: The Magdala Tower, built by Saunière to house his library, which has since become a key location in the mystery of Rennes.

charlatan, and eventually banned from any activities relating to the Priory when he was caught up in a 1993 fraud trial.

This thorough debunking has done little to dent fascination with Rennes and its supposed secrets, and the little village gets more tourists than ever thanks to its tangential association with the Dan Brown book and movie. Today it plays host to an engaging cast of eccentrics and seekers known as "Rennies," including a "Mole of Rennes" who has dug a labyrinth of tunnels that threatens the village's foundations. Rennes's allure no longer relies on the Priory myth, but on its "vibe" as a sort of French Glastonbury.

UNSOLVED EVENTS

This chapter explores unexplained disappearances and mysterious appearances, of people, things, and extraordinary phenomena. Here are individuals whose ultimate fate has often been shrouded in mystery, making them uniquely intriguing yet also troubling. How can someone vanish without trace, and do such disappearances hold some dark significance? Here you will learn of an ancient Persian army swallowed by the desert. You will read of intriguing parallels between the disappearances of the crew and passengers of the *Mary Celeste* in 1872 and the lighthouse keepers of the Scottish island Eilean Mor in 1900.

Alongside these maritime mysteries are several airborne ones, ranging from disappearing planes, passengers, and pilots—like the most audacious skyjacker in history, a man erroneously known as D. B. Cooper, who leaped from a jet in 1971 after extorting $200,000—to the colossal aerial explosion that flattened a forest in Siberia in 1908. Also featured here are two of the strangest appearances in history: Kaspar Hauser, a strange boy who arrived like a character in a novel, and may have had a life story ripped from the pages of one; and the unidentified corpse of a man discovered on an Australian beach, carrying nothing of significance except a tiny scrap of paper bearing the Persian phrase *"Tamam Shud"* ("It is ended").

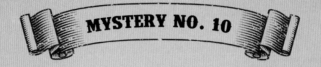

THE MISSING ARMY OF CAMBYSES

Date: 524 BCE
Location: Western Desert, Egypt–Libya border

An army of 50,000 Persian soldiers sent by Cambyses II vanishes without a trace in the desert; 2,500 years later, multiple claims are made about the discovery of its remains.

The eldest son of Cyrus the Great, founder of the Achaemenid Persian Empire, Cambyses II sought to further expand the empire by conquering Egypt. In 525 BCE he employed Arab tribesmen to deposit caches of water across the Sinai desert and successfully brought his huge army into Egypt, defeating the last ethnically Egyptian pharaoh, Psammetichus III. According to Herodotus, the ancient Greek historian who is the primary source for the life of Cambyses, once installed in Egypt he began making plans for further expeditions of conquest—west toward Carthage, south to "Ethiopia" (presumably meaning Nubia), and into the desert to deal with the "Ammonians."

The Ammonians were the inhabitants of the Siwa Oasis, a town deep in the Western Desert, famous for the Oracle of the Temple of Ammon (the Siwan name for the Egyptian god Amun-Ra, whom

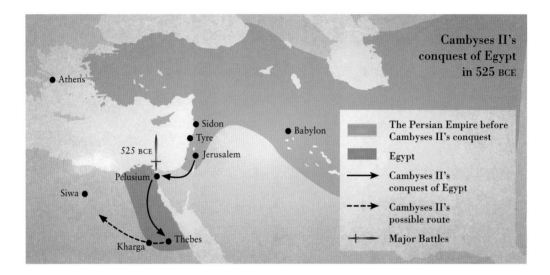

Above: A map showing Cambyses II's conquest of Egypt in 525 BCE, and the possible route that he then took with his army.

the Greeks equated with Zeus). Herodotus relates that Cambyses had arrogantly failed to pay proper respect to the traditions of Egypt and in particular to the proud and powerful guardians of the Temple of Ammon, who as a result had been divining unflattering oracles about him. Cambyses, whom Herodotus paints as a despotic madman, decided to teach them a lesson. In 524 BCE, as he led his army south along the Nile en route to his Ethiopian expedition, Cambyses paused at Thebes to detach a force to send against the Ammonians. The tale that Herodotus relates in Book III of his *Histories* is the sole source for one of the great historical mysteries, and so is worth quoting at length:

> *When he came in his march to Thebes, [Cambyses] detached about fifty thousand men from his army, and directed them to enslave the Ammonians and burn the oracle of Zeus; and he himself went on toward Ethiopia with the rest of his host . . . As for those who were sent to march against the Ammonians, they set out and journeyed from Thebes with guides; and it is known that they came to the city of Oasis [Kharga], inhabited by Samians said to be of the Aeschrionian tribe, seven days' march from Thebes*

across sandy desert; this place is called, in the Greek language, Isles of the Blessed. Thus far, it is said, the army came; after that, except for the Ammonians themselves and those who heard from them, no man can say anything of them; for they neither reached the Ammonians nor returned back. But this is what the Ammonians themselves say: when the Persians were crossing the sand from the Oasis [Kharga] to attack them, and were about midway between [Siwa] and the Oasis, while they were breakfasting a great and violent south wind arose, which buried them in the masses of sand which it bore; and so they disappeared from sight. Such is the Ammonian tale about this army.

TREASURES OF THE SANDS

For modern archaeologists and tomb raiders, the tale of the buried army in the desert is wonderfully tantalizing. What treasures might lie in the sands, undisturbed for millennia and preserved by the arid conditions? None, according to the mainstream view, which is that the story is unreliable. Herodotus was both acclaimed as the Father of History and reviled as the Father of Lies by later ancient historians, and as he himself points out, he is merely repeating a tale he heard as he traveled through Egypt some 70 years after the events he describes. Herodotus paints a picture of Cambyses as a deranged drunk, quite capable of sending a huge army into the desert on a spiteful whim. Alternatively, Cambyses may have planned the attack on Siwa as part of a cunning plan to approach Carthage to the west by an overland route, since the Carthaginian's Phoenician

Opposite: A woodcut by Gustav Dore showing the fate of the army of Cambyses, engulfed by a sand storm.

connections made the coastal route unviable. If the expedition really did take place, however, where should the lost army be sought? The route described by Herodotus has the army marching to Siwa from the oasis known as the Isles of the Blessed, which is today the town of Kharga. In this case they would probably have followed the traditional caravan route via the oases of Dakhla and Farafra, before meeting their end somewhere in the Western Desert. A forbidding, waterless expanse, this includes rocky depressions, plains of salt and dust, enormous sand seas with winds of over 104°F (40°C), and colossal sandstorms. It covers about two-thirds of modern-day Egypt: an area of 262,550 square miles (680,000 sq km)—the combined size of Denmark, Greece, the Netherlands, Norway, Switzerland, Belgium, and Austria.

DESERT EXPLORERS

Below: Egypt's Western Desert: barren and forbidding.

Despite the dangers and difficulties, intrepid explorers have crisscrossed the Western Desert looking for the lost army. Perhaps the most celebrated is the Austro-Hungarian pilot and desert explorer

Count László Almásy, model for the "English Patient" in the book and movie of the same name. In the 1930s, Almásy was part of a crowd of mainly British desert exploration enthusiasts who called themselves the Zerzura Club, who were searching for Zerzura, the Oasis of Little Birds, known from medieval legends. To the astonishment of the club, Almásy located the hidden oasis, turning next to a quest from the pages of his beloved Herodotus: the search for the lost army.

Almásy had earlier seen pottery shards that suggested to him that the army might have buried caches of water jars to create artificial oases, as they had done when crossing the Sinai, but in the desert outside of Farafra all he could find was a series of ancient cairns. A blasting desert wind blew up; Almásy was lucky to escape with his life, and the outbreak of war prevented him from returning to pursue the quest.

BONES AND DOLLARS

In more recent times, a steady trickle of reports have fitfully fanned excitement that Cambyses's army might be found. A 1977 claim that an Egyptian archaeological mission had discovered "thousands of bones, swords, and spears of Persian manufacture" turned out to be a hoax, while a widely reported 2000 claim that an oil-prospecting Helwan University geological team had stumbled upon similar remains came to nothing. More highly regarded expeditions, such as a 1983 National Geographic-sponsored expedition led by Gary Chafetz, found little more than sparse Roman remains and fields of "sand dollars"—fossil sea urchins that might give the illusion of human bones. In 2014, Leiden University Egyptologist Olaf Kaper advanced the theory that the tale of the desert swallowing up the army was invented by Cambyses's successor Darius, as propaganda to cover up the true fate of the troops: they were ambushed and defeated by Egyptian resistance leader Petubastis III, who briefly established a native-ruled kingdom based in Memphis.

— FAR OUT —
THEORIES

Above: Ruins at the oasis settlement of Kharga, from where the army of Cambyses struck out into the desert.

A character named Aly Barakat, described as an Egyptian archaeologist but notorious for claiming that mounds found in Bosnia are ancient pyramids, has been involved in at least two expeditions claiming to have located the lost army, most recently a 2009 trip with Italian brothers Angelo and Alfredo Castiglioni. They produced a documentary showing them poking around a pile of bleached bones and displaying jewelry and metalwork of apparently ancient Persian origin, but their claims are regarded as dubious given that they are shock-documentary producers and that the Egyptian authorities issued a statement specifically refuting their claims as "unfounded and misleading."

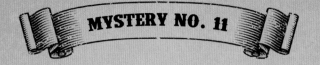

THE LOST COLONY OF ROANOKE

Date: Sometime between 1587 and 1590
Location: Roanoke Island, North Carolina, USA

The disappearance of one of the earliest English colonies in the Americas is a tale of mystery, tragedy, and conspiracy, of strange codes and false trails, and the obscuring sands of time.

In the 16th century, rivers of gold and silver flowing from the New World threatened to overturn the balance of power in Europe. The Spanish Empire grew rich and powerful. Isolated and threatened, Protestant England nurtured colonial ambitions of her own. Companies of merchants and noblemen launched missions to explore, exploit, and stake claims to North American territory, among them the syndicate put together by Sir Walter Raleigh, the Queen's favorite. In 1584 Raleigh obtained a license to lands in the largely notional territories of Virginia, and in 1585 he sent a force under Ralph Lane to establish the first English colony in the Americas, on Roanoke Island in what is now North Carolina. Dwindling food supplies and hostile relations with most of the Native Americans led to the abandonment of the colony a year later, and a force of 15 men left to maintain Raleigh's title disappeared, with evidence that they had been killed or driven off.

THE WHITE COMPANY

In 1587 a second wave of colonists arrived, led by John White,
who had served as official artist on the previous colonizing
attempt. On July 22, 90 men, 17 women, and 11 children came
ashore at Roanoke Island. Although their original intent had been
to set up on more favorable territory on the mainland, Simon
Fernandez, the captain in charge of the ships that brought them,
refused to take them any further. It has since been alleged that
Fernandez was in the pay of Sir Francis Walsingham, Elizabeth
I's spymaster and a court rival of Raleigh's, and that Walsingham
conspired at every step to thwart and doom the nascent colony.
White's company set about rebuilding the colony, and just over
a month later his daughter gave birth to Virginia Dare, the first
English child born in the Americas. By this time things were

Below: Theodore
de Bry's 1591 map
of Virginia, showing
both Roanoke and the
territory of the Croatans.

already going wrong; poor relations with neighboring tribes had led to the murder of one colonist. The settlers voted to send White back to England to secure support and supplies, and on August 27 he set off, promising a swift return.

Above: An image from a 19th-century history book, showing the landing of the colonists at Roanoke.

Events conspired against White, however, particularly the war between England and Spain and the subsequent Armada, and it was not until August 1590 that he was able to return, although as a passenger rather than in command. Coming ashore with a landing party, White "sounded with a trumpet a Call, & afterwardes many familiar English tunes of Songs, and called to them friendly," but there was no sign of the colonists. All that was left behind was a palisade of timber that had been erected after White's departure, and a few heavy lumps of metal. It seemed that everything else had been packed up and removed. The only clue as to where were two odd inscriptions. On a tree near the shore were the letters "CRO," and on one of the palisade timbers the word "CROATOAN." To White, the implication was clear: the colonists had gone to take refuge with a friendly tribe of Native Americans, the Croatans of nearby Hatteras Island, leaving, as agreed, "a secret token" of their intent. If they had been in distress the inscription was to have included a Maltese cross, but no such mark was seen. Indeed, the plan had always been for the colonists to move from Roanoke to a site "50 miles into the maine [inland]," so to find them gone was not in itself mysterious. Tragically for White, an attempt to visit Hatteras Island and search for his family and the other settlers was thwarted by storms, and he was forced to return to England, never to see them again.

FALLEN IN BATTLE

Below: A marker erected to show the site of the Lost Colony, also mentioning Virginia Dare.

Subsequent search parties were sent, but several were sidetracked and none made positive contact. When the Jamestown colony was set up in Virginia, further efforts were made, and John Smith, the leader of the new colony, gathered native accounts of white men

encountered—and killed—around Chesapeake Bay. The hostile Native American chief Powhatan, father of Pocahontas, told him that he had attacked and killed a group of white men to the south, showing Smith "a musket barrell and a brass mortar, and certain pieces of iron that had been theirs."

There were sporadic further attempts to locate the lost colony and a theme developed of claimed encounters with "white Indians" familiar with English and Christianity, widely assumed to be the descendants of the White company's intermarriage with their Native American hosts. But the validity of these claims is dubious, and the original colony on Roanoke has been lost under shifting sands. So the mystery remains: what became of the lost colony?

A SECRET LOCATION

Some of them may well have followed the original plan to relocate to the mainland, to a site previously identified by Raleigh's explorers as the source of a valuable natural resource: sassafras, extracts of which had great value medicinally and in brewing (it was used to make root beer). Accounts of the early explorers make much play of "secret commodities [at] a secret location," and the paper trail of early maps and land titles leads precisely to a spot "50 miles into the maine." Sassafras exploitation was probably the prime motive behind Raleigh's entire project, so it is highly plausible that the colonists moved to the "secret location." A map by White himself suggests it may have been a Native American site at the head of the Alligator River named "Tramaskecooc."

The most widely accepted theory about the fate of the colonists is that they intermingled with the Croatans and the combined group moved inland. Research undertaken by the Lost Colony Center for Science and Research, using old land deeds, suggests that Croatan descendants held title to land at a site called Gum Neck, which seems to correspond exactly to the site of Tramaskecooc, precisely 50 miles inland from Roanoke. While the mystery of

— FAR OUT —
THEORIES

The unsolved disappearance of the colonists has generated a range of outlandish speculations. Inevitably alien abduction is among them, but more plausible theories include the conspiracy theory that Walsingham plotted to undermine Raleigh's colony (see page 71), suggested by Lee Miller in her book *Roanoke: Solving the Mystery of the Lost Colony*. It is also possible that the Spanish captured the colonists. The Roanoke colony was a direct challenge to the Spanish colonization of North America. The Spanish colony at San Augustin in Florida got word of the English settlement and in 1588 a small expedition was sent north to look for—and possibly destroy—the Roanoke colony, but it came back empty-handed and the Spanish governor concluded that the colony was failing or gone.

Above: A portrait of Sir Walter Raleigh; although he never visited the Lost Colony, its fate may have been linked to his own.

the lost colonists may not be definitively solved, it seems that a plausible explanation has emerged for what happened to them, at least initially. Their long-term fate, however, remains unclear. Were they all killed by Powhatan or others? Are their descendants still around today?

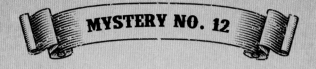
THE AMBER ROOM

Date: 1701
Location: St. Petersburg, Russia

A priceless collection of exquisite amber panels, making up one of Russia's most treasured artifacts, was looted by the Nazis and never recovered; its whereabouts remain "one of the greatest art mysteries of the century."

The history of the Amber Room dates back to Prussia, 1701, when an ambitious court sculptor and architect saw his chance to catch the eye of a young queen. Andreas Schlüter had fallen out of favor with Queen Sophie Charlotte, the wife of Prussian King Frederick I, and was seeking a way to win back her patronage. In the cellars of the Royal Palace Schlüter stumbled across a huge store of amber, fossilized pine resin known as the Gold of the North and traditionally collected on the Baltic shore of Prussia.

Schlüter conceived the idea of fitting out in amber a room in one of the palaces that Sophie Charlotte was having refurbished. He recruited master craftsmen, who had to use a new method of working with amber to realize his ambitious vision. Fragments of amber were heated, soaked in an infusion of honey, linseed, and

resin, and molded into flat leaves, which could then be pieced together like a mosaic or stained-glass window, on a backing of wood covered in gold or silver leaf. The intention was to create a set of panels and boards of amber, which could then be fitted onto the walls of a room, together with other suitably magnificent ornaments, to create an unprecedented spectacle that would blaze with golden light.

Above: Part of the replica Amber Room in the Catherine Palace, suggesting the ornate magnificence of the original.

WORTH ITS WEIGHT IN GIANTS

The deaths of Queen Sophie Charlotte and Frederick I meant the project remained incomplete, and in 1716 Frederick William I gave the panels to the visiting Russian tsar, Peter the Great, who was known to love amber. Peter demonstrated his gratitude with a return gift of fifty-five giants (his regiment of men all over six feet [180 cm] tall), and the room was brought to the new city he had founded, St. Petersburg. It remained in storage until 1743, when Empress Elizabeth revived the project and had the room installed at the third Winter Palace, then moved to the Catherine Palace in Tsarskoye Selo (a village outside St. Petersburg, home of several imperial palaces). It was only finally completed in 1770 by Catherine the Great, who added new panels and ornamentation, including four Florentine stone mosaics.

STOLEN BY THE NAZIS

The Amber Room dazzled and awed visitors to the palace through the 19th century, the fall of the monarchy, and the Russian Revolution. Along with the other treasures of the imperial palaces, it was displayed to the Russian people and cared for by curators until World War II. With the Nazis advancing rapidly toward Leningrad (as St. Petersburg was now called), head curator Anatoly Kuchumov was ordered to pack up what he could for evacuation to the east. To his dismay, he could not find a way to take down the amber panels without breaking them, and in desperation he had them covered with fake walls, in the hope that the Germans would pass over the greatest art treasure in Russia.

Below: Königsberg Castle in 1925; later it would house the Amber Room before being gutted by fire at the end of World War II.

The ruse failed, and the Nazis quickly managed what Kuchumov had been unable to do, dismantling the room and shipping it back to Königsberg, ancient seat of the Teutonic Knights and, the Germans considered, the spiritual home of the Amber Room. Here it was displayed in Königsberg Castle until the Russians began to close in, when it was packed up once more and plans to ship it elsewhere for safekeeping were then discussed.

PROFESSOR BUSOV INVESTIGATES

On May 31, 1945, just three weeks after the German surrender
(but more than six weeks after the fall of Königsberg), Professor
Alexander Brusov of the State Historical Museum in Moscow
arrived in Königsberg to find out what had happened to the
Amber Room. To his dismay he found the city in ruins, and most
of the castle a burnt-out shell. Penetrating to the cellars, Brusov
discovered that an intense fire had swept through this part of the
castle. Amid the ashes were the carbonized remains of three of the
four Florentine mosaics from the Amber Room—of the rest of the
room, there was no sign.

The evidence of the cellars looked bad, but Brusov was determined
to explore all options. He knew from interrogation of Germans
who had worked at Königsberg Castle that the Amber Room had
been packed up with the intention of shipping it off to a safer
spot. The former curator of the castle's art collection led him to a
bunker across town but there was no sign of the room. Eventually
he returned home with the gloomy conclusion that the room had
probably been destroyed in the castle fire—a casualty of war.

But Kuchumov, the Catherine Palace curator who had looked
after the room for so many years, refused to accept this. With
KGB backing, he savaged Brusov's efforts and findings, destroying
the Professor's career, and launched his own investigations in
Königsberg, uncovering evidence that the Nazis had scouted
locations in the Prussian countryside, and also in more distant
parts of Germany, as possible safehouses for the storage of looted
art. Kuchumov followed the trail of the room to Berlin, but
without success, and later he and other Russian investigators, led
by the KGB, returned yet again to Königsberg. Over four decades,
the former German city, now a Russian enclave and naval base
called Kaliningrad, was thoroughly explored, tunneled, excavated,
and turned over, but no trace of the room has ever been found.

A FRUITLESS SEARCH

Meanwhile, Germans from both sides of the Iron Curtain had joined the hunt, inspired by articles—carefully placed in the international press by Communist intelligence agencies—that insisted the room had survived the war and awaited rediscovery. After reading the articles, and encouraged by his bosses, who knew that repatriating the Amber Room would curry favor with their masters in Russia, Stasi agent Paul Enke became an expert on all things to do with the Amber Room, eventually publishing 1986's *Bernsteinzimmer Report*, the best-known book on the subject. Enke chased the room to various castle art depositories across East Germany, but found the Soviets peculiarly uncooperative when it came to accessing important documents. He came up empty-handed, though convinced the answer was within reach.

Other clues and rumors have led to the Amber Room being sought in lakes and mines all over Europe, but the only traces that have ever been found are the fourth mosaic, stolen from Leningrad by a Wermacht soldier in 1941 and kept secret by his son until the late 1990s, and a chest of drawers also stolen before the room left Russia. In 2003, a replica of the Amber Room was installed in the Catherine Palace at Tsarskoye Selo to mark the 300th anniversary of the founding of St. Petersburg. It took over 20 years and more than 6.5 tons (6 tonnes) of amber to create, and was partly funded by German donations.

THE UNPALATABLE TRUTH

In 1999, British investigative reporters Catherine Scott-Clark and Adrian Levy started to research the fate of the Amber Room, publishing the results in their 2004 book *The Amber Room*. After diligently tracing all the false leads and wrong turns taken by everyone from Kuchumov to Stein (see box on page 81), they came to a startling conclusion. The evidence clearly suggested that the Amber Room had indeed been destroyed by fire in the cellars of Königsberg Castle in 1945, just as Brusov had feared, but

— FAR OUT —
THEORIES

In West Germany, strawberry farmer and amateur historian George Stein took up the hunt for the Amber Room after previously helping to repatriate other art treasures to Russia. A suspect letter purporting to be from an SS officer led him to believe that the room had been shipped out of Königsberg to an old mining complex in Lower Saxony, although searches here proved fruitless. Over the next 25 years the hunt for the room would destroy Stein's family—his wife committed suicide and his children disowned him—and eventually his sanity. He supposedly disemboweled himself with a scalpel in mysterious circumstances in 1987, after having

Above: Another view of the replica Amber Room, the treasure that has inspired heartache and obsession.

become convinced that the room had been shipped off to America after the war.

this conclusion had been suppressed by Kuchumov, who did not want to believe it, possibly for fear that he would be blamed for not taking down the panels and saving the room when the Nazis invaded. The Soviet state had gladly seized upon Kuchumov's version because it served to cover up an unpalatable truth—the fire that destroyed the room had been set by Soviet troops, engaged in an orgy of looting and destruction. The articles about the room were deliberate disinformation, and all the many KGB and Stasi investigations simply smokescreens.

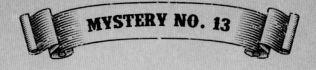
KASPAR HAUSER

Date: 1828–1853
Location: Germany

An untraceable youth appears from nowhere, claiming to have grown up in isolation. He becomes a celebrity but is killed in mysterious circumstances, leaving an enduring enigma.

Kaspar Hauser, a youth who appeared in Nuremberg in 1828, was apparently a feral boy, whose past proved impossible to trace. He became very famous and the focus of suspicions that he might be the lost heir of the Grand Duke of Baden, before being killed in mysterious circumstances. In fact, almost everything about Kaspar was mysterious: his origins, upbringing, abilities, character, and demise, aptly summarized by the epitaph on his gravestone, which read: "Here lies Kaspar Hauser, riddle of his time. His birth was unknown, his death mysterious." According to a 1996 estimate, he has been the focus of at least 3,000 books and over 14,000 articles.

The story began with the appearance of a short young man (estimated to be in his late teens) in the streets of Nuremberg on May 26, 1828. Speaking a rough dialect of Bavarian, he asked to be directed to a cavalry officer's household since he had letters addressed to the man. The letters claimed that their bearer was the son of an unnamed trooper, who had been commended to the care of a poor peasant, who in turn was now commending him to the care of the military. In typical fashion for the Kaspar Hauser tale, these letters became the source of controversy. It was suggested that they were both written by a single hand, although this was countered by others; it was also claimed that one of the letters was clearly a fake penned shortly before delivery, because it was addressed to an officer in Nuremberg, even though the man in question had not lived in the city in 1812 when the letter was supposedly written.

Above: A portrait of Kaspar Hauser from 1830. He appears robust for someone supposedly reared on bread and water in a lightless cell.

The boy could write his name as "Kaspar Hauser," but appeared to have only a limited vocabulary. He was short, and his legs were covered in scars, but he seemed relatively robust. Installed in the town jail, for want of anywhere else to put him, Kaspar began to unfold a remarkable tale. He claimed to have been raised entirely without human contact in a small cell with boarded-up windows, fed only with bread and water, yet he could walk, was in decent health, and showed no signs of vitamin or sunlight deficiency. Given tuition, he learned to talk, read, and write with remarkable speed, belying the status of "idiot" or simpleton that had at first been attached to him. He seemed to have unnaturally sharp senses; it was said that he could see in the dark, and he seemed to be hypersensitive to electricity, as during a thunderstorm. Public sympathy saw him awarded a small pension, and he became the subject of numerous pamphlets and newspaper articles as word of his mysterious origins spread. There even appeared, in 1829, his autobiography, with graphic details of his awful upbringing.

MANY CATS ARE THE DEATH OF THE MOUSE

Some of those charged with his care and education grew exasperated with what they saw as his increasing laziness and conceit, and with his apparently uneasy relationship to truthfulness. Stories of Kaspar's origins, particularly the luridly Gothic suggestion that he was the true heir to a Grand Duchy (see box on page 85), began to circulate, and if he did not author these rumors he seemed to enjoy and play up to them. In October 1829, at around the same time that his notoriety was beginning to dim, and after falling out with his guardians, he was found with a gash to his forehead, which he claimed had been inflicted by a mystery assailant, although many suspected him of having inflicted the wound himself. In April 1830, after another falling out with another guardian, he suffered a mild self-inflicted gunshot wound, supposedly by accident.

By now Kaspar had become internationally famous and for a time was taken up by a visiting English nobleman, Philip Henry, Lord Stanhope, a friend of the Baden family. Stanhope encouraged Kaspar to think he would be taken back to England, but in fact the Englishman appears to have tired of him, leaving him in the care of a harsh schoolmaster in December 1831. A year later, again following an argument with his guardian, Kaspar was killed. On December 14 he staggered home, clutching his side where a deep stab wound had pierced his lung and liver, and managed to gasp out the words: "man . . . stabbed . . . knife . . . Hofgarten . . . gave purse . . . Go look quickly . . ." When police later searched the Hofgarten park in which Kaspar claimed to have been stabbed by an unknown assailant, they found a black wallet or purse containing a note written in mirror writing, which read: "Hauser will be able to tell you how I look, where I came from, and who I am. To spare him from this task I will tell you myself. I am from

—FAR OUT—
THEORIES

A popular theory about Kasper Hauser was that he was the child of Karl, Grand Duke of Baden, who had died in 1818, apparently without surviving male issue after two sons died at birth, so that his title passed to an uncle. Supposedly, a cunning aunt had swapped a dying peasant baby for Karl's healthy son, Kaspar, who was then reared in isolation, ignorant of his true patrimony. A 2002 DNA analysis of samples from artifacts of Kaspar Hauser showed that he might well have been related to the House of Baden.

Right: A statue of Hauser, clutching his letter of introduction, in the German town of Ansbach where he died.

. . . on the Bavarian border . . . My name is MLO." Three days later, Kaspar died; even his last words were enigmatic: "Many cats are the death of the mouse . . . Tired, very tired, still have to take a long trip." Detractors claimed Kaspar had stabbed himself to win sympathy and attention but misjudged and inflicted a fatal wound. Supporters claimed Kaspar had been assassinated by dark forces intent on suppressing the truth about his origins. The truth remains unknown.

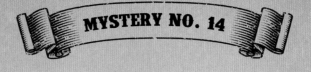

THE *MARY CELESTE*

Date: 1872
Location: Atlantic Ocean, off the Azores

The *Mary Celeste* was an American brig found in the middle of the ocean, abandoned by her crew despite being seaworthy enough "to sail around the world." Her name has since become a byword for mysterious disappearances.

The *Mary Celeste* (often misspelled nowadays as *Marie Celeste*) had begun life in Nova Scotia in 1860 as the *Amazon*, but had suffered a long history of misfortune and tragedy. She had run aground, caught fire, gone through multiple captains, and been associated with several bankruptcies and deaths. She was salvaged and in 1868 was given her new name.

By 1872 she was under the command of Benjamin Spooner Briggs, who also owned a share in the vessel, and in early November he oversaw the loading in New York of a cargo of 1,701 barrels of alcohol for shipment across the Atlantic to Italy. Accompanying him on the fateful trip would be his wife and daughter, along with a crew of seven. After leaving New York on November 5, none of these people would ever be seen again.

ABANDONED AT SEA

Exactly one month later, on December 5, the crew of the British ship *Dei Gratia* spotted a vessel adrift in the Atlantic, off the Azores. Her sails were in a poor state, and after hailing the crew but receiving no reply, Captain Morehouse sent across a party to investigate. They searched the whole ship but found not a soul. The ship itself was remarkably seaworthy; it had lost the foresail and upper foresail, which had been blown off their yards, but other sails were either stored, furled, or set. Some of the rigging was fouled or blown away, and some of the hatch covers had been taken off and tossed aside, although the main cover was still battened down. There was not much water sloshing around in the hold but plenty in barrels for drinking, and most of the provisions were intact and unspoiled. There appeared to be no reason for her

Below: An engraving of the *Mary Celeste* as she appeared when found abandoned; note that most of the sails and rigging are in good order.

abandonment, and the ship's log in Captain Brigg's cabin offered no explanation; the last entry read, "Monday, 25th [November]. At five o'clock made island of St. Mary's bearing ESE. At eight o'clock Eastern point bore SSW six miles [3 km] distant."

It was evident enough what had happened to the crew, at least initially: the yawl (a small boat normally lashed to the main hatch) was missing, and part of the railing along one side of the ship had been removed, obviously in order to launch the yawl. Also missing from the ship were the chronometer, sextant, bill of lading, and navigation book; in other words, the items that would be grabbed in the event of a hurried abandonment. But this simply begged a far greater mystery: what would drive a captain to abandon a perfectly seaworthy ship in the middle of the ocean, and pile into a small boat with seven crew and his wife and two-year-old daughter?

Captain Morehouse of the *Dei Gratia* sent across a skeleton crew to get the *Mary Celeste* back to Gibraltar. He and his men could expect a rich salvage prize, especially given the excellent condition of the ship and its intact cargo. Unfortunately,

Opposite: Arthur Conan Doyle as a young man; his story based on the *Mary Celeste* mystery was one of his first literary successes.

Below: A map showing the largely parallel courses of the *Mary Celeste* and *Dei Gratia*, until their convergence on December 5th.

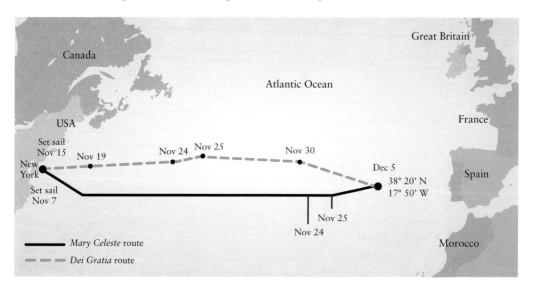

-88-

however, these were precisely the factors that would pitch the men of the *Dei Gratia* into a maelstrom of accusation, suspicion, and prosecution. The British attorney general in Gibraltar, Frederick Solly-Flood, smelled a rat on learning of the particulars of the case. He initially suggested that the crew of the *Mary Celeste* had got drunk on the cargo and murdered the captain and his family, but this theory foundered on the fact that the cargo was of denatured (chemically altered) alcohol, which would cause violent sickness before intoxication. Flood then proposed that Morehouse and his crew were guilty of murder and piracy, and although they were eventually cleared of all suspicion, Flood's antics had succeeded in publicizing the mystery of the *Mary Celeste* far and wide. Newspapers picked up the story, and in 1884 it became the subject of a popular short story, *J. Habakuk Jephson's Statement*, one of the earliest works of Arthur Conan Doyle. Doyle misspelled the ship's name as *Marie Celeste* and, although fictional, his version of the story was widely repeated as a factual account.

NO HUMAN INGENUITY

In July 1887, the United States Consul in Gibraltar, Horatio Sprague, wrote that: "This case of the *Mary Celeste* is startling, since it appears to be one of those mysteries which no human ingenuity can penetrate sufficiently to account for the abandonment of this vessel and the disappearance of her master, family and crew . . ." Human ingenuity has, nonetheless, made many attempts to penetrate the mystery. Discounting the more far-fetched theories (see box on page 91), it is obvious that what needs explaining is not the question of *how* the crew came to leave the ship—clearly they got into the yawl—but *why*? Presumably they thought the ship was in danger and that the yawl was the safest option. The cargo of alcohol was an obvious threat; if the crew believed that fumes had leaked out and might be about to ignite and cause an explosion, they would have abandoned ship.

One theory is that the ship was hit by a waterspout—a small tornado—which led to a sudden drop in pressure above decks. This might have caused the smaller hatches to pop off, fooling the crew into believing that expanding alcohol vapor was to blame (also explaining the disposition of the hatches). Alternatively, the fall in pressure could have caused a malfunction in the gauge that showed the water level in the hold, making it appear that the ship had taken on masses of water after being buffeted by the waterspout. The modern-day sea captain David Williams has a theory that the *Mary Celeste* was hit by waves from an undersea quake, and this panicked the crew into abandoning ship.

Whatever the reason, the crew scrambled to launch and board the yawl, pausing only to grab essential navigation equipment. Any relief they felt on seeing that the ship was not exploding or sinking would have been short-lived, because presumably the line holding them to the *Mary Celeste* broke for some reason, leaving them to perish at sea. On May 16, 1873, a newspaper in Liverpool reported that two rafts had washed ashore on the coast of Spain, to which were lashed corpses and an American flag. Although this was not investigated at the time, it has been suggested that these were the last remains of the crew of the *Mary Celeste*. The ship herself lived on for more than a decade, making multiple crossings of the Atlantic, although maintaining her reputation as a jinxed ship. In 1885 she was run aground and burned by her last owner,

—FAR OUT—
THEORIES

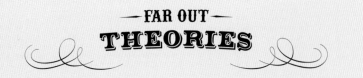

In the early 20th century, a popular theory attributed the disappearance of the crew to the depredations of a giant octopus, kraken, or similar sea monster. Later the kraken was replaced by aliens, with the now popular theory that the crew of the *Mary Celeste* were abducted by aliens. Another culprit blamed is the vortex or strange force of the Bermuda Triangle, although this hypothetical area does not in fact extend as far as the Azores. None of these theories explains why the yawl, navigation instruments, and ship's papers also went missing.

Pl. XXVI.   *T. 2. P. 256.*

Denys-Montfort del.   **LE POULPE COLOSSAL.**   *E. Voysard S.*

Right: This famous early 19th-century illustration of a giant squid attacking a ship represents contemporary beliefs about marine perils.

Gilman C. Parker, in an insurance fraud. Although Parker escaped conviction on a technicality, the curse of the *Celeste* seems to have caught up with him as he died in poverty and disgrace.

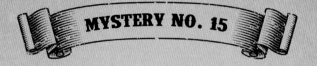

THE EILEAN MOR LIGHTHOUSE KEEPERS

Date: 1900
Location: Flannan Isles, Outer Hebrides, Scotland

In the winter of 1900, three lighthouse keepers were found to have inexplicably vanished without a trace from their post on the remote Scottish island Eilean Mor.

On December 26, 1900, a ship arriving at the lighthouse at Eilean Mor received no answer to its horn or signal flare, and no one was waiting at the landing stage to greet it. Captain James Harvey had sent the relief keeper, Joseph Moore, to check out the lighthouse, which he found empty. One of the men's jackets was still on its hook, and all the clocks had wound down and stopped. Typical recountings of the tale add the provocative details that a half-eaten meal lay on the kitchen table and a chair had been overturned, as if someone had sprung to their feet in alarm. These telling details are in fact pure fabrication; as we shall see, this has come to be a feature of the case. Moore and some of Harvey's crew searched the small island, but there was no trace of the three missing keepers, Principal Keeper James Ducat, second assistant keeper, Thomas Marshall, and occasional keeper Donald Macarthur. Harvey sent a telegram to Edinburgh, alerting the Board that "A dreadful accident has happened at Flannans."

Eilean Mor was fertile ground for ghost stories and superstition. A remote and storm-swept island, it is the largest of the Flannan Isles, a group of barren islands rising steeply from the Atlantic Ocean about 21 miles (34 km) northwest of Gallan Head, on the westward tip of the Hebridean island of Lewis. The islands are named for St. Flannan, a 7th-century Irish bishop who supposedly built the island's small chapel, the ruins of which remain there today, and who was quite possibly the last person to live there until the lighthouse was built in 1899.

Above: The Eilean Mor lighthouse today; it is unmanned.

THE LOGBOOK OF DOOM

Many popular accounts include several eerie details, most strikingly the last entries in the lighthouse logbook, attributed to the assistant keeper, Thomas Marshall. On December 12 he supposedly wrote: "Sea lashed to fury. Stormbound 9pm. Never seen such a storm . . . Ducat irritable . . . 12pm: storm still raging . . . Ducat quiet. Macarthur crying." On December 13 the logbook recorded that Macarthur was praying, and later that there was

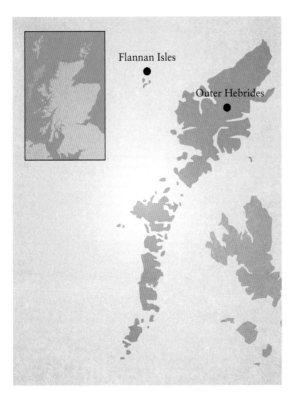

Flannan Isles

Outer Hebrides

Above: The Flannan Isles, Atlantic outpost of the Outer Hebrides.

"Gray daylight. Me, Ducat, and Macarthur prayed." The last entry, dated December 15, read simply: "1pm. Storm ended. Sea calm. God is over all." Perhaps the most disturbing detail is that, despite the record of the logbook, the weather was calm on December 12–15, with storms not setting in until the 17th.

In fact, none of the eerie details stand up to investigation. Researcher Mike Dash points out that an assistant keeper would not have made all the entries, and he certainly would not include impressions, thoughts, and insubordinate remarks. In fact, log entries were initially made on a chalkboard before transfer to the book, so the last few entries would not have been written down. Dash traced the first appearance of the log entries to an August 1929 edition of pulp-fiction magazine *True Strange Stories*. Similarly bogus is the contention that the weather was fine when the keepers disappeared; in fact, stormy weather and high seas had battered the island at this time.

The most likely explanation for the disappearance of the three men was one similar to that which Harvey suggested in his original telegram: "Poor fellows they must been blown over the cliffs or drowned trying to secure a crane or something like that." Muirhead found no evidence of sudden abandonment of the lighthouse; the kitchen was clean and tidy and there were no half-eaten meals on the table. He did find evidence, however, near one of the island's landing platforms, that a huge wave had

—FAR OUT—
THEORIES

The fictional additions to the story of the missing keepers have prompted various theories, including alien abduction and mystical transportation to the "Otherworld." Antiquarian and UFO guru John Michell developed an elaborate theory based on Martin's writings, suggesting that Eilean Mor (often erroneously translated as "Island of the Dead," when in fact it simply means "Big Island") was the home of the fairies or Little Folk, to whom human sacrifices were ritually offered. By shipping the men to the island and shutting them up in a tower, the theory went, the ancient ritual had unwittingly been revived, opening a portal for the eldritch beings to claim their latest sacrificial victims. An even more fantastic theory was invented wholesale by children's author Carey Miller, who

Above: Another view of the Eilean Mor lighthouse, showing the path down to one of the landing stages.

wrote, "an unseen force on the island of Eilean Mor would not tolerate intruders and got rid of them. They say that when Joseph Moore flung open the door of the lighthouse and called out the names of his friends, three enormous black birds the like of which have never been seen before launched themselves from the top of the tower and flew out to sea."

knocked down a heavy crate, dislodged a huge rock, and torn a life buoy from its ropes, even though it was 110 feet (33 m) above sea level. The most likely explanation is that one or more vast waves had carried the men off to their doom.

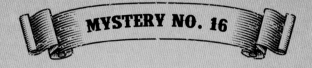
THE TUNGUSKA EVENT

Date: 1908
Location: Siberian taiga forest, Russia

In 1908, a colossal blast leveled a forest in Siberia. Scientists, ufologists, and conspiracy theorists alike are still arguing about whether it was a meteorite, a comet, or something far stranger.

At seven in the morning, local time, on June 30, 1908, a vast fireball blossomed above the taiga forest in a remote part of Siberia near the Tunguska River. A man at a trading post 40 miles (64 km) away was knocked to the ground by a huge shock wave, feeling as though he were on fire. "Suddenly in the north sky," he related, "the sky was split in two and high above the forest the whole northern part of the sky appeared covered with fire . . . At that moment there was a bang in the sky and a mighty crash . . . The crash was followed by a noise like stones falling from the sky, or of guns firing. The earth trembled." The tremors could be recorded on the other side of the globe.

Extraordinarily, lights were seen from thousands of miles away. *The New York Times* reported from Berlin that "Remarkable lights were observed in the northern heavens on Tuesday

Left: The shattered remnants of a forest charred and blasted by the Tunguska explosion.

and Wednesday nights, the bright diffused white and yellow illumination continuing through the night until it disappeared at dawn . . . ," and a few days later claimed that in London it was "Like Dawn at Midnight . . . people believed that a big fire was raging in the north of London . . . shortly after midnight, it was possible to read large print indoors . . . it would be interesting if anyone would explain the cause of so unusual a sight."

WILDEST EXPECTATIONS

An explanation would be a long time in coming. The extreme remoteness of the area, coupled with the unsettled state of Russia in the early 20th century, meant that an investigative expedition, led by Leonid Kulik, the chief curator for the meteorite collection of the St. Petersburg museum, would not be launched until 1921. Even then, Kulik was turned back by extreme conditions, trying again in 1927. Kulik first researched local newspaper archives, reading tales of epic fireballs and local people hearing a sequence of 14 "thunders." On April 13 Kulik finally reached the site of the blast, recording that "The results of even a cursory examination exceeded all the tales of the eyewitnesses and my wildest expectations." He found a 21,500-square-foot (2,000-sq-km) zone of devastation, with some 80 million trees flattened outward in a radial pattern around 30 miles (50 km) across, except in the center where the trees stood upright, stripped of their branches—leading to this area being termed the "Telegraph Pole Forest." Conspicuously absent was the central impact crater, in which Kulik had hoped to find a valuable meteorite. There were some small impact craters suggestive of meteorite fragments. Amazingly, no humans had been killed, although many reindeer had died.

WRATH OF THE GODS

Local informants blamed a pagan god, who had apparently blasted the earth in anger, but Kulik deduced that a meteor had exploded in the sky before impact. The conventional explanation for the Tunguska Event is that an asteroid around 120 feet (37 m) across, weighing 615,000 tons (560,000 tonnes), and traveling at around 33,500 mph (54,000 kph), exploded under the pressure and heat of its own shock wave, at a height of around 28,000 feet (8,500 m). The explosion was equivalent to roughly 10–20 megatons of TNT, around 1,000 times more powerful than the Hiroshima atomic bomb, although a 2008 supercomputer simulation led by physicist Mark Boslough at Sandia National Laboratories in Albuquerque, New Mexico, suggests the asteroid may have been only half as large, exploding with a yield of around 3–5 megatons.

In 2007, a team led by Luca Gasperini of the University of Bologna claimed to have identified Lake Cheko in the Tunguska region as the impact crater of a large fragment of the event meteorite, and although this is controversial, there is other circumstantial evidence for a meteoric air burst, including the eyewitness reports, the distribution of the fallen trees, and the presence of particles such as nanodiamonds in sediments in the area. According to Mark Boslough, "the [scientific] community has pretty much accepted the view that it was a carbonaceous [rocky] asteroid."

— FAR OUT —
THEORIES

Above: New growth on a tree blasted by the explosion, photographed 30 years later.

The absence of hard evidence that the Tunguska Event was caused by a meteorite has led to a proliferation of candidates. A small comet was first suggested in the 1930s, independently, by astronomers F. J. W. Whipple and I. S. Astapovich—since comets are made of ice, this would account for the absence of traces after the explosion, as the comet would have vaporized itself. More exotic astronomical objects suggested include antimatter and a mini black hole. After World War II, some noted similarities between the "Telegraph Pole Forest" and the trees left standing limbless at Hiroshima, after the intense atomic blast had stripped the branches before they could transmit the force to the trunks. This suggested to some that the Tunguska Event was a nuclear explosion—and since humans had not invented this technology in 1908, this must have had an extraterrestrial origin. Conspiracy theorists link the event to claims Nikola Tesla had developed earthquake-causing, wireless-transmission energy weapons. German astrophysicist Wolfgang Kundt and others point to a kind of geological "fart," termed a "Verneshot" after the author of *A Journey to the Center of the Earth*, involving the explosive release of highly pressurized gas from beneath thick basalt.

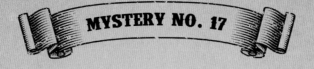

AMELIA EARHART

Date: 1937
Location: Somewhere in the South Pacific

The most famous aviatrix of all time, Amelia Earhart was a global celebrity when she made a daring attempt on the round-the-world flight record; her unsolved disappearance in the Pacific has since sparked a rash of rumors and speculation.

On July 2, 1937, Earhart and her navigator Fred Noonan went missing over the Pacific as they neared the end of their circumnavigation attempt in a Lockheed L-10E Electra twin-engine plane. They had already flown three-quarters of the way around the world when they set off on midnight of July 2 to fly 2,556 miles (4,113 km) from Lae, New Guinea, to Howland Island, a tiny coral island that had been converted into a landing strip. The US Coast Guard cutter stationed there to meet them picked up garbled radio transmissions, but the plane never arrived. It later transpired that the charts Earhart and Noonan were using were wrong.

A huge air–sea search was launched, initially focusing on the most obvious scenario: that Earhart, unable to find the island, had run out of fuel and ditched somewhere to the northwest of Howland

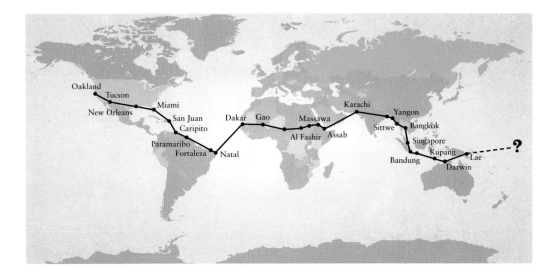

Above: Earhart's progress around the world, and the possible route her plane took after her final departure point in New Guinea.

Island, along the line of travel from her last transmission: "We are on a line of position 157/337, will repeat this message, we will repeat this message on 6210 kcs [i.e. switching to a different frequency]. Wait." The "line of position" was the line between the two bearings, and Earhart was probably zigzagging across it in a search pattern. Even as ships were steaming to the search zone, further transmissions were picked up, raising hopes that the aviators were still alive with intact radio equipment. The US Navy focused its search on the area where some of the signals appeared to come from: the uninhabited Phoenix Islands to the southeast of Howland. Navy planes criss-crossing the area picked up a solitary lead: "signs of recent habitation" on Gardner Island, one of the Phoenix group, though no one was visible. On July 18, the search was called off.

Although rumors and legends developed claiming that Earhart had survived the crash or had been engaged on a secret mission (see box on page 105), serious researchers accept that she and Noonan perished after their plane ran out of fuel over the Pacific. But did they ditch at sea, as the official verdict suggested, in which case the Electra would have sunk and might still be resting on the seabed,

3 miles (5 km) down, or did they make it to an island—probably one of the Phoenix Islands—only to die there when they were not rescued? Both possibilities have been seriously investigated.

Above: Amelia Earhart, pictured in front of her Lockheed Electra in 1937.

SEARCHING THE SEABED

A 2002 expedition by the Nauticos Corporation, experienced deep-sea search and recovery experts, focused on the explanation originally given by the captain of the Coast Guard cutter. He reasoned that since Howland Island was at the limit of the Electra's range, on failing to find it, Earhart and Noonan would soon have run out of fuel and ditched the plane, hoping to make it out in one piece in their life raft and get rescued. Nauticos president, David Jourdan, argued that they had a good chance of finding an intact plane: "The deep ocean is a very preserving environment. There are no currents or tides at that depth, and no human interactions that could have degraded what's there. Biological remains would have disintegrated quickly, but metals survive. We expect the plane to look pretty much like it did when it went down." Nauticos sent expeditions in 2002 and 2006, using vessels equipped with sophisticated seabed imaging equipment to scan 630 square nautical miles (2160 sq km) of an area near Howland Island, but these have so far come up empty-handed.

THE CASE FOR NIKUMARORO

The major group involved in ongoing investigations into the fate of Earhart and Noonan is The International Group for Historical Aircraft Recovery (TIGHAR), which has sent a number of expeditions to the tiny Pacific island of Nikumaroro, formerly known as Gardner Island. They have amassed a wealth of circumstantial evidence for the possibility that Earhart landed the Electra at Nikumaroro and survived for at least a short time afterward. First, they showed that the plane was fitted with extra fuel tanks that would have allowed Earhart and Noonan several more hours in the air than formerly believed. Assuming that they

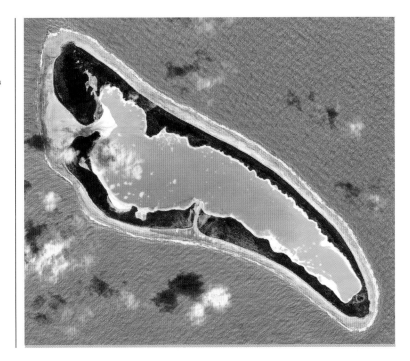

Right: TIGHAR used satellite images of Nikumaroro Island like this one to help them identify possible locations for Earhart's landing.

were proceeding southeast on the 157/337 line Earhart reported in her last transmission, they could easily have reached Nikumaroro, which was within visual range of this course.

TIGHAR theorize that Earhart put the plane down on a stretch of coral visible at low tide, on which the SS *Norwich* had run aground in 1929. After landing, the aviators might have had time, before the plane was swamped by the incoming tide, to make a final radio transmission, which would account for a message picked up on the island of Nauru on the evening of July 2, 1937, on the same frequency that Earhart had previously said she would switch to, which supposedly sounded like Earhart. The plane would eventually have been washed off the reef, and one target of the TIGHAR investigations is to find traces of the wreckage on the seabed off the island. But there is also evidence that Earhart and Noonan survived for a while as castaways on a desert island. Colonists who attempted to settle on the island in 1938 reported finding human bones, a sextant case, and the sole of a woman's shoe. The bones themselves have been lost, but their description potentially matches a Caucasian female of Earhart's size. TIGHAR themselves have found fragments of metal panels that match ones known to have been fitted in the Electra.

Direct physical confirmation of their theory has proven elusive for TIGHAR. Scans of the seabed have pinpointed an anomaly near the location on the reef where they believe the plane came down, but a 2015 expedition to examine this anomaly ended in frustration when technical problems put out of action their remotely operated vehicle. Searches on the island itself also failed to find anything new, but both TIGHAR and Nauticos have vowed to continue their multimillion-dollar search programs.

—FAR OUT—
THEORIES

Above: Earhart pictured in happier days; could she have been a secret agent for the US?

One of the many Earhart conspiracy theories claimed that the US Navy had taken advantage of the search for the aviatrix as a pretext to overfly the Marshall Islands, a Japanese mandate zone where it was suspected they were illegally building military bases. Popular legend also claimed Earhart's disappearance was not merely an accident. Evidence included suggestive radio transmissions picked up from parts of the Pacific after the crash, "eyewitness" reports of Earhart and Noonan in custody, and even photos of the pair. It has also been suggested that the US Government holds secret documents on Earhart, which it refuses to declassify; this may be related, conspiracy theorists claim, to the theory that the US authorities covered up Earhart's capture and death at the hands of the Japanese to avoid a public backlash. In fact, the story of the classified documents is bogus and, similarly, the supposed reports and photos turned out to be fake.

Nonetheless, searches have been launched at two sites where Japanese prisoners were held. The soldier St. John Naftel served on the Pacific island Tinian just after its liberation from the Japanese in 1944. He says he was shown Earhart's and Noonan's graves, but a 2004 mission failed to find any evidence. Another location searched fruitlessly was the site of a wartime Japanese prison on the Pacific island Saipan, supposedly identified as the place of Earhart's death by a French consul, who in 1937 wired the US State Department to alert them.

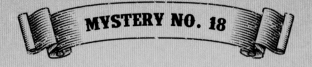

THE BERMUDA TRIANGLE AND THE DISAPPEARANCE OF FLIGHT 19

Date: 1945
Location: Atlantic Ocean between Bermuda, Florida, and Puerto Rico

The Bermuda Triangle is a legendary region of the Atlantic Ocean, associated with mysterious disappearances of ships and planes—especially a US Navy training patrol, which vanished without a trace in 1945.

A triangle of ocean, with its northern apex at Bermuda, its southwest apex in southern Florida, and its southeastern apex at around 40 degrees longitude near Puerto Rico, became known in the second half of the 20th century as the Bermuda Triangle—aka the Devil's Triangle, the Hoodoo Sea, the Graveyard of the Atlantic, and the Triangle of Death. According to the legend (or is it myth?) of the Bermuda Triangle, as many as 50 ships and 20 aircraft have mysteriously disappeared while traveling through this region, often associated with reports of anomalous phenomena such as compasses ceasing to work, radio interference, yellow fogs, and meteorological and optical irregularities.

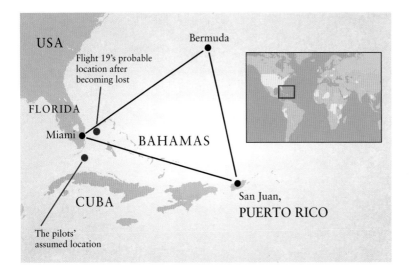

USA

Bermuda

Flight 19's probable
location after
becoming lost

FLORIDA

Miami

BAHAMAS

CUBA

San Juan,
PUERTO RICO

The pilots'
assumed location

Left: A map showing the
Bermuda Triangle;
the location Flight 19's
pilots assumed they had
flown to upon realizing
they were lost; and their
probable actual location.

The concept of the deadly triangle was first introduced in 1964, in
the mainly fictional magazine *Argosy*. It really took off, however,
with the bestselling 1974 book *The Bermuda Triangle* by Charles
Berlitz, and his is the classic treatment. The founding tragedy of
the Bermuda Triangle myth was the disappearance on December
5, 1945, of a routine training flight of five Navy bombers. Flight
19 included an experienced instructor and four experienced pilots;
their mission that day was to practice a navigational maneuver
that would see them fly about 125 miles (200 km) out to sea from
their base at Fort Lauderdale (23 miles [37 km] north of Miami)
and then return. The weather was mostly fair, with good visibility.

At 4pm a radio message between two of the pilots was picked
up, making it clear that they were lost. The flight leader
complained that his compass was not working, and according to
the popular version of the tale, he also said, "everything seems
wrong . . . strange . . . even the ocean doesn't look as it should."
The similarities to the eerie logbook entries of the Eilean Mor
lighthouse keepers (see page 92) are striking, in more ways than
one. Radio contact was lost and search and rescue teams sent to
the area found no trace of pilots or wreckage. One of the planes

sent out to look for Flight 19, a PBM patrol plane, also vanished. Other disappearances linked to the Bermuda Triangle include the SS *Marine Sulphur Queen*, a tanker that went missing in 1963, and the nuclear submarine USS *Scorpion*, lost in 1968.

ANOTHER ANGLE ON THE TRIANGLE
The problem with Bermuda Triangle theories is that many of the classic disappearances are not that mysterious. The region has some notable geological anomalies, including undersea volcanoes and, in particular, a zone of magnetic anomaly where true north and magnetic north exactly coincide; in most of the rest of the world, navigators are taught to allow for the deviation between them. The spooky radio transmissions of Flight 19 were invented, but the pilots did complain about their compasses. Perhaps the lead navigator was not sufficiently briefed on the magnetic anomaly of the true–magnetic north alignment and hence got lost. Having lost their bearings out at sea, and with their compasses and radios not working properly, the pilots of Flight 19 had little chance. The June 1973 edition of *Naval Aviation News* reported: "Former TBM pilots that we questioned express the opinion that the crew of an Avenger attempting to ditch at night in a heavy sea would almost certainly not survive the crash . . . The aircraft most probably broke up on impact and those crewmen who might have survived the crash would not have lasted long in cool water."

As to the missing PBM, the airplane had a poor reputation as a highly flammable "flying gas tank." A merchant ship off Port Lauderdale reported seeing "a burst of flame, apparently an explosion," passing through an oil slick at a time and place that matched the presumed location of the PBM. The missing tanker, *Marine Sulphur Queen*, was similarly flammable since it carried tanks full of molten sulfur, and a nearby banana boat reported to the Coast Guard that they had run through a cloud of acrid smoke at just this time. As for the USS *Scorpion*, it was located

—FAR OUT—
THEORIES

The popular myth of the Bermuda Triangle goes far beyond mundane explanations. The supposed reports of strangeness that precede vanishings have been taken as evidence of a dark force or bizarre paranormal phenomenon—perhaps some kind of vortex that sucks vessels into another dimension. Alien abduction is another favorite, represented in Spielberg's movie *Close Encounters* when the alien mothership disgorges confused Navy fliers from the 1940s, clearly intended to be the missing airmen of Flight 19. Other candidates include a giant octopus-like sea monster (see the *Mary Celeste*, page 86); giant bubbles of methane released by seafloor mudslides; eruptions of volcanic gas; tsunamis; and waterspouts.

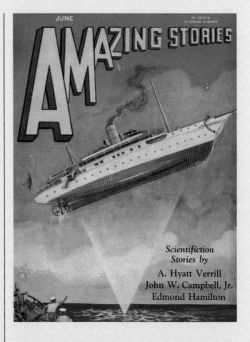

Scientifiction
Stories by
A. Hyatt Verrill
John W. Campbell, Jr.
Edmond Hamilton

Above: A 1930 issue of pulp magazine *Amazing Stories*, featuring one of the earliest tales of an anti-gravity vortex in the Atlantic.

around 400 miles (645 km) southwest of the Azores, a long way from even the broadest conception of the Devil's Triangle. Its sinking was attributed to mechanical failure. In fact, statistically speaking, the Triangle—one of the world's busiest regions for shipping and air travel—is no more dangerous than anywhere else, and explanations such as sudden storms, freak waves, and navigational error can account for all the known losses of vessels.

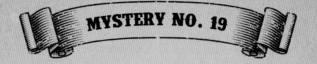

THE TAMAM SHUD MURDER

Date: 1948
Location: Adelaide, South Australia

A body found on an Australian beach may have been a murder victim, but his identity, the murder weapon, the motive, and the murderer all remain unknown in this case filled with tantalizing clues and oddities.

Also known as the Somerton Beach mystery or the riddle of "the Unknown Man," the Tamam Shud murder is one of the most perplexing cases in history. On December 1, 1948, a smartly dressed man was found propped up against the sea wall on Somerton Beach near Adelaide, in South Australia. He had been noticed the previous evening, lying in the same position and apparently drunk, smoking a cigarette, but now he was clearly dead. The coroner was unable to determine the cause of death or even whether he had been murdered, but considered it likely he had been poisoned, although extensive analysis failed to find any trace of poison. An expert suggested that the poisons digitalis and strophanthin, available from pharmacists, would quickly break down after use, making them undetectable. Other clues, such as the pattern of blood pooling in the corpse, suggested that perhaps he had died elsewhere and been moved.

ORANGE THREAD

The identity of the corpse proved impossible to ascertain. All of the labels had been cut out of his clothes, including those in a suitcase that was eventually found at the Adelaide train station, with the exception of some items bearing the name "Kean" or "T Keane"—no one of this name could be tracked down, and it was assumed by police that the name tags had been left precisely because the mystery man was not Kean (or Keane). Details such as the stitching of his jacket and the direction of stripes on his tie suggested that the man had come from America. On his person the man had had a train ticket from Adelaide to the beach, a pack of chewing gum, and no form of identification. One of his trouser pockets had been repaired with orange thread. He also had a pack of Army Club cigarettes containing seven cigarettes of another brand; it has been suggested that if he was poisoned, the mystery toxin was administered by way of a cigarette, which might explain the odd substitution of brands.

The coroner made a particular point of noting the unknown man's highly developed and extremely unusual calf muscles, and his wedge-shaped toes. These were said to be reminiscent of an athlete, or someone who wore high-heeled or dancing shoes, suggesting that the man had been a ballet dancer. Four months after the initial investigation, a more

Below: The grave of the unknown man from the Tamam Shud mystery, located in the West Terrace Cemetery in Adelaide, Australia.

detailed search revealed a tiny pocket in the waistband of the man's trousers—probably a fob-watch pocket—in which was found a rolled-up scrap of paper bearing, in distinctive and elaborate type, the phrase *Tamam Shud*. This is the phrase that ends the classic Persian poem *The Rubaiyat of Omar Khayyam*, and means "It is ended" or, more colloquially, "The end." One obvious interpretation was that this was a kind of suicide note, and that the unknown man had killed himself.

THE *RUBAIYAT* CODE

A search was launched for the copy of the *Rubaiyat* from which the paper had been torn, and in July 1949 a man who lived near Somerton Beach came forward to say he had found the book in the back of his car, apparently tossed through the window. The copy contained more clues and yet more baffling enigmas. In invisible ink on the back cover were inscribed five lines of code:

WRGOABABD

MLIAOI

WTBIMPANETP

MLIABOAIAQC

ITTMTSAMSTGAB

These have since resisted all attempts at decryption, not least because they present too short a text. Many have assumed they are a cyphertext, where letters in the message have been transposed for others, but an Australian Naval Intelligence analysis found that they statistically matched the most common initial letters of words in English, suggesting that in fact the code is an acrostic, where each letter is the first of a word. For instance, MLIAOI might be code for "Meet Luke In Adelaide Once Invited." Such a code would be impossible to decrypt.

THE JESTYN CONNECTION

Also written in the book was the signature *"Jestyn"* and a phone number, which police traced to a nurse, now known to be Jessica Ellen Thomson (née Harkness), who lived near Somerton Beach. Thomson admitted that her nickname was Jestyn, and that she had given a copy of the *Rubaiyat* to a man who was not her husband: one Alfred Boxall. Detectives believed that they had finally identified their corpse, but it turned out that Boxall was alive and well and still had his copy of the *Rubaiyat*.

Thomson was called in for further questioning and shown a cast of the dead man's face; Detective Sergeant Lionel Leane was very struck with her reaction, recalling that she was "completely taken aback, to the point of giving the appearance she was about to faint." Yet she insisted she did not know him, and never revealed anything further. One of the leading experts on the case, Professor Derek Abbott, claims that whenever interest in the case flared up Thomson would contrive to go on holiday or make herself unavailable, and she took her secrets to the grave. Abbott discovered that Thomson had a son, Robin, and says that there was a strong physical resemblance between him and the unknown man, also noting that he became a ballet dancer. One suggested scenario is that the unknown man committed suicide after visiting Thomson and being told he could not see his son.

Above: A page from an illuminated manuscript of *The Rubaiyat of Omar Khayyam,* with calligraphy and ornamentation by William Morris and illustrations by Edward Burne-Jones.

Tracking down the edition of the *Rubaiyat* possessed by the unknown man proved incredibly difficult. Eventually it was found to be similar to an edition by an obscure New Zealand publisher—but not identical. Abbott learned that another dead man from around the same period was found with an edition of the *Rubaiyat*, and that this book too proved to be a one-off. It was labeled as a seventh edition of the Methuen version of the book, except that Methuen had published only five editions. To experts on spycraft, these anomalies suggest that the books may have been created as one-time pads—source books for unbreakable codes.

SPY GAMES

Thomson's daughter, Kate, refused for a long time to discuss the case, but in 2013 she told an Australian TV station that she believed her mother could speak Russian, and had confessed to knowing the Somerton Beach man and claimed that the whole business was over the heads of the local police. The clear implication was that Thomson had lived a double life and had been a spy at some point, and in fact Boxall was also known to have worked in intelligence during the war. Although Adelaide might seem an unlikely spot for Cold War high drama, it was not far from top-secret testing grounds at Woomera, where the British were developing rocket technology and would later test nuclear weapons. Speculation aside, the Tamam Shud case remains as much of a mystery as it was in 1958, when the South Australia coroner finally published his conclusions, admitting: "I am unable to say who the deceased was . . . I am unable to say how he died or what was the cause of death."

— FAR OUT — THEORIES

Above: A British de Havilland Venom WK436 in flight.

A recent effort to crack the code of the Unknown Man has focused on micro-writing, where minuscule letters are concealed within larger ones. Since the original book was disposed of by police in the 1950s, these efforts rely on magnified photographs, and have been widely derided by many familiar with the case. However, Gordon Cramer, a former UK detective, claims to have identified micro-writing spelling out the word "Venom X4621," similar to the number of a tender document related to the British de Havilland Venom aircraft, which was in development in 1948 and hence might have been a topic of interest for spies. Cramer also claims that below this are the letters "LZ 5056," which he suggests is the flight number of a Bulgarian Airlines flight from Sofia to London. Professor Derek Abbott is skeptical that the resolution of the photos is great enough to allow such detail to be made out.

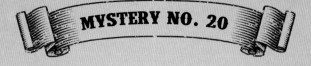

D. B. COOPER

Date: 1971
Location: Somewhere over Washington State

The only unsolved aircraft hijacking in US history featured a mystery man who demanded $200,000 and a parachute, and then leaped from the plane mid-flight. Neither he nor the money have ever been found.

Celebrated as a daring "skywayman" and adopted as an anti-establishment icon, D. B. Cooper perpetrated one of the most irresistible unsolved crimes of the 20th century. Notable today for its continuing cultural legacy and the plethora of claims made for the true identity of the man at its heart, perhaps the first thing to note is that he was not called D. B. Cooper.

On November 24, 1971, a man wearing a suit and raincoat bought a ticket at Portland airport, under the name Dan Cooper. A reporting error, possibly based on an early and quickly ruled-out suspect in the subsequent police investigations, meant that he has become erroneously known in perpetuity as D. B. Cooper. Cooper booked himself onto a Northwest Orient airlines flight to Seattle. On boarding the plane he put on sunglasses, ordered a whiskey, smoked a cheap brand of cigarette, and gave the stewardess a note, written in capital letters: "I HAVE A BOMB IN MY BRIEFCASE. I WILL USE IT IF NECESSARY. I WANT YOU TO SIT NEXT TO ME. YOU ARE BEING HIJACKED." Asked by a stewardess whether he had a grudge against Northwest Airlines, he replied, "No, miss. I just have a grudge."

Cooper told the captain that when the plane landed in Seattle he wanted to be given $200,000 and four parachutes. In return he would allow 36 people to leave the aircraft. The FBI met his demands and the plane took off again, crewed by just the pilot, co-pilot, and a single stewardess. Cooper ordered them to fly the plane to Mexico at 200 mph (320 kmh), at an altitude of 10,000 feet (3,000 m). The crew were instructed to stay in the cabin, although the stewardess observed Cooper strapping something—presumably the money—to his body. At 8pm Cooper manually lowered the rear stairway of the plane, and at 8:13pm, about half an hour after takeoff, over the lower Cascade Mountains about 25 miles (40 km) from Portland, he leaped from the aircraft, never to be seen again.

Below: A map showing the area near the Washington–Oregon border where detectives searched for Cooper.

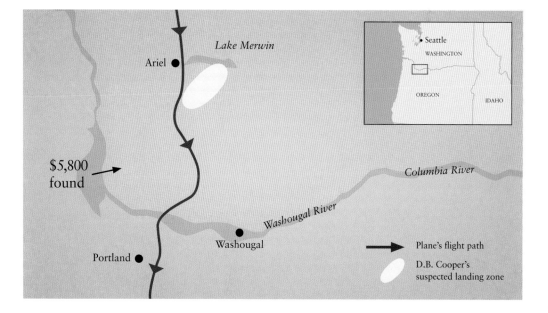

ON THE TRAIL OF DAN COOPER

The military recreated his skydive and estimated that his likely drop zone was around Lake Merwin near Ariel, in Washington State. Drinkers in a local tavern supposedly saw someone hiking up the road that night, in the midst of a storm, but a manhunt found no trace of Cooper. The only leads were the clip-on tie he had left on the airplane, from which a later generation of investigators were able to obtain some DNA samples, and partial fingerprints Cooper had left behind. Subsequently, in 1978, hunters near Castle Rock, north of Lake Merwin, discovered the information placard from the rear staircase of the hijacked flight, while in 1980 a boy on a beach on the Colorado river found in the sand three packets of ransom money, totalling $5,800. The other $194,200 has never been recovered. In 2008, not far from Lake Merwin, a piece of parachute was found, believed to be from a chute used by Cooper.

Debate rages over whether Cooper knew what he was doing in pulling his barely believable stunt of leaping from an airliner at 10,000 feet (3,000 m). Geoffrey Gray, author of the 2012 book *Skyjack: The Hunt for D. B. Cooper*, believes that Cooper's choice of parachute "tells us a lot about who he was." By opting for a military chute over an easier civilian one, Gray argues, Cooper showed that he had probably had military parachute training, possibly in Korea. The FBI, on the other hand, disagreed. According to Special Agent Larry Carr, in charge of the ongoing case: "We originally thought Cooper was an experienced jumper, perhaps even a paratrooper . . . [but] we concluded after a few years this was simply not true. No experienced parachutist would have jumped in the pitch-black night, in the rain, with a 200-mile-an-hour wind in his face, wearing loafers and a trench coat . . . He also missed that his reserve chute was only for training and had been sewn shut . . . a skilled skydiver would have checked [that]."

Carr, and the rest of the FBI, believe the most likely fate of Dan Cooper was that he died, either as the result of his madcap stunt,

— FAR OUT —
THEORIES

Minnesota man Lyle Christiansen believed that his brother Kenneth had been Dan Cooper, after he made a near-confession on his deathbed. Ken Christiansen had been a paratrooper who later went to work for Northwest Orient Airlines, and he had supposedly bought a house with cash just after the skyjack. The family of a man called Lynn Doyle Cooper, a tough outdoorsman familiar with the Pacific Northwest region, suggested that he was the culprit, recalling him turning up to Thanksgiving 1971 covered in bruises, claiming to have been in a car accident. Perhaps the most extraordinary claim regards Barbara Dayton, a transgender woman who had been a pilot and parachutist before undergoing gender reassignment surgery, starting in 1969. It is suggested that it was easy for her to revert to a male persona for the heist,

Above: The FBI composite image of Dan Cooper.

before once more adopting her female persona as the perfect cover afterward. The FBI maintain that DNA profiling and other checks have ruled out every candidate yet suggested.

or shortly afterward from exposure to harsh conditions. Possibly his body was washed down the Columbia River and out to sea, never to be found. Despite this strong probability, several people have been identified as Dan Cooper (see box).

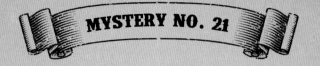

THE DISAPPEARANCE OF MALAYSIA AIRLINES FLIGHT MH370

Date: 2014
Location: Somewhere in the Indian Ocean

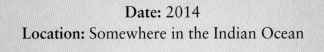

When Flight 370 from Kuala Lumpur disappeared in March 2014, 239 people went missing with it. The fate and location of the plane remain a mystery, prompting a diverse crop of conspiracy theories.

Just after midnight on March 8, 2014, Malaysia Airlines Flight MH370 took off from Kuala Lumpur, heading for Beijing in China. On board were 227 passengers from 15 nations (mostly Chinese) and 12 Malaysian crew. At 01:19 Malaysian time the Captain, Zaharie Ahmad Shah, made the final voice contact, although previous radio contacts had been made by the First Officer, Fariq Abdul Hamid. Three minutes later, the plane disappeared from the radar screens of air-traffic controllers, although military radar continued to track the flight. This track showed that MH370 deviated from its set flight path, executing a U-turn and flying across the Malay Peninsula, along the border between Thailand and Malaysia. At 02:22, over the Andaman Sea, the plane flew out of range of Malayan military radar.

OUT TO SEA

Once the flight's disappearance was reported, initial search efforts concentrated on the area near its last radio contact, and later, after the military tracking was revealed, on the Andaman Sea. It then transpired that satellite communications company Inmarsat had exchanged "pings" with transponders on the aircraft, and analysis of these showed that the plane was still flying at 08:19, heading into the southern Indian Ocean. In January 2015 the Malaysian government formally declared that MH370 had accidentally crashed, and that the plane had come down somewhere in the Indian Ocean, presumably when it ran out of fuel.

On July 29, 2015, a piece of aircraft wing was found on the shore of Réunion island in the Indian Ocean, and later formally identified as part of the wreckage of MH370. Its discovery is consistent with the assumption that the plane crashed in the

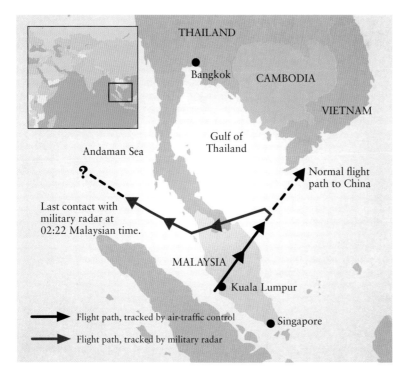

southern Indian Ocean, since the two sites are linked by ocean currents that carry flotsam and jetsam. The flaperon that washed up is the only physical trace of MH370 yet discovered, despite the largest and most expensive search in aviation history. At the time of writing, the search operation is covering an area identified as the most likely location by British pilot Simon Hardy, whose reconstruction of the most likely flight path has been widely publicized and deemed highly credible. Hardy even supplies a specific set of coordinates, S39 22' 46" E087 6' 20", although the authorities disagree with his claim that the plane was splash-landed in a controlled manner, and hence possibly sank intact. The official line is that a transmission from one of the plane's engines suggests it was out of fuel, in which case the plane would have crashed into the ocean and probably broken up.

CRUCIAL QUESTIONS

The continued absence of physical traces of the plane and an explanation for its change of course and doomed flight path has bred a vast array of conspiracy theories. Such theories need to account for several questions. Why did at least one of the flight crew execute the changes in course? Did other crew or passengers try to do something about it, and if not, why not? Why did none of the passengers try to use their mobile phones to call out? The least sensational theories assume that the passengers and most of the crew were almost instantly knocked out, probably by explosive depressurization of the aircraft. One theory is that this was linked to an electrical fire, in response to which one of the pilots tried to reroute to the nearest landing place, before being overcome. Another mainstream theory is that one of the pilots perpetrated the disappearance and crash as a form of suicide, in similar fashion to the actions of Andreas Lubitz, who crashed Germanwings Flight 9525 on March 24, 2015.

— FAR OUT —
THEORIES

According to a CNN poll in 2014, a tenth of respondents thought it possible that "space aliens, time travelers, or beings from another dimension" were involved in the plane's disappearance. Other theories fall into two broad camps: the plane was shot down, or it never really crashed. British writer Nigel Cawthorne has developed a theory that MH370 was accidentally shot down as part of a military training exercise between the United States and Thailand, and that they covered it up by removing all traces of the wreckage. Alternatively, the plane was shot down by the US because it had been hijacked by terrorists intending to crash it into the American air base on the Indian Ocean island of Diego Garcia.

Diego Garcia also features in theories that the plane was spirited away by the Americans, Israelis, or others, and used for a "false flag" operation: a copy of the 9/11 attacks, which could be blamed on Iran or another enemy. The subsequent bringing down of Malaysian Airlines

Above: MH370's sister airplane, an identical Boeing 777.

Flight MH17 over Ukraine in July 2014 led to claims that MH17 was actually MH370, and its downing was faked to implicate Russian-backed separatists (if this were true, what happened to MH17?). Rupert Murdoch suggested the plane had been hijacked by jihadists intending to "make trouble for China," and flown to northern Pakistan "like Bin Laden." North Korea and Russia have also been blamed; the plane had just enough fuel to make it to Central Asia, leading to speculation that it was flown to Baikonur Cosmodrome, which is leased from Kazakhstan by Russia.

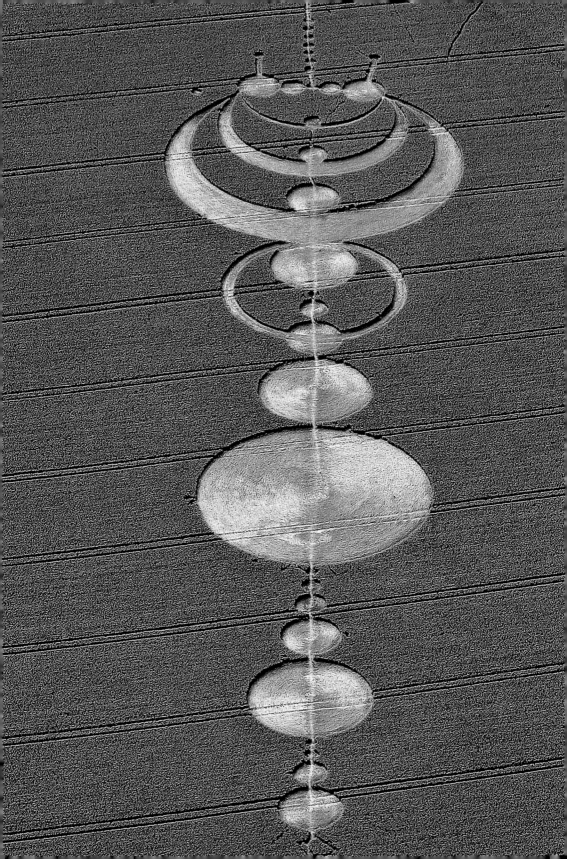

STRANGE SIGHTINGS

To what extent does a mystery reside in the witness? This chapter explores accounts of strange phenomena, from demonic creatures apprehended by medieval peasants to odd lights in the sky and bizarre monsters. Some phenomena seem to have left physical traces, like the odd bipedal hoofprints that appeared overnight in heavy snowfall in southwest England in 1855, sparking wild rumors that the Devil had left his mark. Others seem to be flesh-and-blood creatures, whether lake-dwelling prehistoric survivors, or hominid relic species, popularly known as Bigfoot or the yeti. But even the most apparently prosaic of these cryptid animals, the out-of-place panthers and pumas sighted in Britain and beyond, turn out to be hedged about with high strangeness, marking them out as denizens of the paranormal rather than natural world.

In this chapter you will meet Spring-Heeled Jack, an improbable leaping fiend in tight-fitting white oilskins. You will also learn of visions of the Blessed Virgin Mary, bestowing great secrets on peasant children or exuding fluids from statues. And you will discover the history of claimed visitations from outer space, in the shape of UFOs, and investigate what may be the best evidence yet of contact from another civilization, known as the Wow! signal because of the handwritten note that first identified it in 1977.

Left: Crop circle glyphs in California in 2003, proving that the phenomenon is not restricted to southwest England.

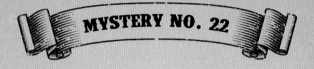

SPRING-HEELED JACK

Date: 1837–1904
Location: United Kingdom

Spring-Heeled Jack, the Victorian-era bogeyman of urban legend, took many forms, but was always distinguished by an incredible jumping ability.

Spring-Heeled Jack was the name given by the popular press to a masked fiend who terrorized Victorian Britons for nearly 70 years, but who was almost certainly a figment of the cultural imagination—what sociologists call a "collective delusion." Reports of the apparition varied widely, but all shared one common feature—the mystery assailant could perform superhuman leaps, as though he (or it) had springs on his heels. Spring-Heeled Jack was not the first of such urban legendary bogeymen, and certainly not the last.

Mystery assailants are a surprisingly common feature of societies all over the world and throughout history. They feature in social panics that tend to follow a similar pattern. A minor but unusual report of a frightening encounter with otherworldly elements stimulates further reports, which spark into life a media frenzy. This in turn disseminates both the threat of attack and the cultural vocabulary used to articulate experiences, becoming a self-sustaining process. The only physical consequences of supposed encounters prove to be exaggerated, unrelated, or potentially self-inflicted, and pinning down witnesses with genuine first-hand reports proves to be impossible. Eventually, the panic dies down without resolution, although it can easily flare up again at a different location.

The first recorded encounters with Spring-Heeled Jack came in December 1837, with the *Morning Chronicle* reporting the appearance of "some scoundrel, disguised in a bear-skin, and wearing spring shoes . . . jumping to and fro before foot passengers in the neighbourhood of Lewisham." Apparently the locals had taken to calling him Steel Jack. In the next few weeks, similar apparitions were reported in various parts of London, with widely varying descriptions including "in the shape of a white bull," "in the form of a white bear," "dressed in polished steel armour," and "in the form of an immense baboon six feet high with enormous eyes." Though not always present, a white or shiny costume was emerging as another common thread.

Above: The classic image of Spring-Heeled Jack, with his tight-fitting oilskin costume and demonic attributes, from a penny dreadful of 1837.

THE UNMANLY VILLAIN

In January 1838, the rumpus gained wider credibility when *The Times* reported on a letter read out by the Lord Mayor of London, Sir John Cowan, which claimed that "some individuals . . . have laid a wager that a mischievous and foolhardy companion . . . durst not take upon the task of visiting many of the villages near London in three disguises – a ghost, a bear, and a devil . . . the unmanly villain has succeeded in depriving seven ladies of their senses." The following month brought perhaps the definitive encounter, when Jane Alsop, a teenager from London's East End, heard what she thought was a policeman crying from the street: "For God's sake, bring me a light, for we have caught Spring-Heeled Jack here in the lane." When she opened the front door and handed the cloaked figure a candle, he revealed his full monstrosity, with, according to *The Times*, "eyes that resembled red balls of fire," a helmet of some sort, and a costume, "which appeared to fit him very tight [and] seemed to resemble white oil skin." This ghastly apparition "vomited forth a quantity of blue and white flames from his mouth" and clawed her, "tearing her gown with his claws, which she was certain were of some metallic substance."

The attack on Jane Alsop gained widespread notoriety, and London was in such a ferment that winter that the Duke of Wellington organized special patrols to reassure the populace. The legend of Spring-Heeled Jack "went viral," and he was sighted around the country over the next few decades. In the 1880s, for instance, he was a particular presence in the Midlands; according to a typical report from the *Birmingham Post* in September 1886: "First a young girl, then a man, felt a hand on their shoulder, and turned to see the infernal one with glowing face, bidding them a good evening." By this time, Jack had crossed over into fiction and folklore. He was the star of several penny dreadfuls (cheap illustrated serials) and even appeared in plays. His name became a generic term for robbers who made a quick getaway, and he became a bogeyman with which parents could frighten recalcitrant children. "Jack" was always a popular nickname for shady characters, but in the late 1880s acquired a darker association with the Ripper murders. Perhaps the last recorded sighting of Spring-Heeled Jack was in September 1904, when newspapers in Liverpool reported a figure seen "jumping over a building in William Henry Street."

— FAR OUT —
THEORIES

An extraordinary but enduring explanation offered for Spring-Heeled Jack was the suggestion that he was an extraterrestrial spaceman. The helmet and strange costume were his spacesuit, and his powerful leaps evidence that he came from a planet with higher gravity than Earth. One of the earliest proponents of the spaceman theory was British actor Valentine Dyall in a 1954 article for *Everybody's Magazine*, in which he argued, "It is significant that a high proportion of those who saw [Spring-Heeled Jack] were convinced that he was not of this world, but either a spirit or a visitor from some distant planet." This suggestion was taken up by a correspondent to the magazine, Inman Race of Sheffield, who contended that "a

Above: Could Spring-Heeled Jack have been a visitor from outer space?

Being, reared on a planet where gravity was far greater than on earth would be able to leap colossal distances on THIS planet . . . I suggest that the alleged monster was a visitant from Space who had been marooned."

Who or what was Spring-Heeled Jack? The 1838 letter to the Lord Mayor had suggested a suspect from "the higher ranks of life," and in his book *The Legend and Bizarre Crimes of Spring-heeled Jack*, author Peter Haining suggests the culprit was the Marquess of Waterford, a well-known practical joker. But the most plausible explanation is that Jack was an example of a collective delusion.

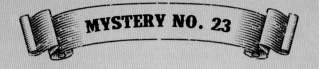

THE DEVIL'S FOOTPRINTS

Date: 1855
Location: Devonshire, England

It was midwinter in Victorian England, and bipedal hoofed tracks appeared overnight in fresh snow, traversing fields and gardens, unimpeded by walls or rivers. Was the Devil to blame?

Heavy snow fell on the night of February 7–8, 1855, in south Devon (in the southwest of England). It stopped at around midnight, and at first light the next morning, roughly six hours later, people across the countryside and settlements between Topsham and Totnes, including the towns of Lympstone, Exmouth, Teignmouth, and Dawlish, noticed strange tracks in the snow, meandering in an unbroken course over a distance of more than 100 miles (160 km).

The first reports of the tracks appeared in the February 17 edition of the local newspaper, in a letter to the editor: "Sir, Thursday night, the 8th of February, was marked by a heavy fall of snow, followed by rain and boisterous wind from the east, and in the morning frost. The return of day-light revealed the ramblings of some most busy and mysterious animal, endowed with the power of ubiquity, as its foot-prints were to be seen in all sorts of unaccountable places – on the tops of houses, narrow walls, in gardens and court yards, enclosed by high walls and palings, as well as in the open fields."

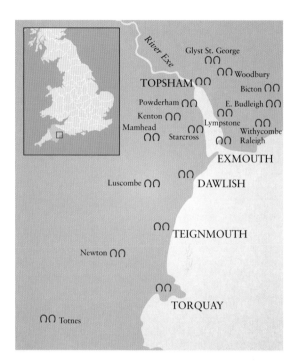

The letter went on to describe the prints, which appeared "more like that of a biped than a quadruped": "the steps are generally eight inches in advance of each other, though in some cases twelve or fourteen, and are alternate like the steps of a man, and would be included between two parallel lines six inches apart. The impression of the foot closely resembles that of a donkey's shoe, and measures from an inch and a half to (in some cases) two inches and a half across, here and there appearing as if the foot was cleft, but in the generality of its steps the impression of the shoe was continuous and perfect; in the centre the snow remains entire, merely showing the outer crust of the foot, which, therefore, must have been convex."

Above: A map showing all of the points in south Devon where the hoofprints were reported to have appeared.

Although the tone of the letter was jolly enough, it added the chilling detail that "The creature seems to have advanced to the doors of several houses, and then to have retraced its steps . . ." The Rector of Clyst St. George, the Reverend H. T. Ellacombe, who went on to become one of the principal investigators of the phenomenon, recorded a further disturbing facet: "[it was] as if the snow had been branded with a hot iron . . . to the ground, which was everywhere visible, tho' the snow in the middle part did not appear to be touched." Perhaps inevitably, dark suspicions of the Devil's hand were being entertained.

THE NATURE OF THE BEAST?

People in the district were genuinely frightened. According to *Trewman's Exeter Flying Post*, which described the affair as "an excitement worthy of the dark ages," a group of tradesmen from Dawlish were sufficiently alarmed to arm themselves with "guns and bludgeons" and follow the tracks to Luscombe, Dawlishwater, and Oaklands. "At length, after a very long and weary search, they returned as wise as they set out." Henrietta Fursdon, the daughter of the Vicar of Dawlish, later recalled "seeing the footprints, and my terror as a child of the unknown wild beast that might be lurking about, and the servants [who] would not go out after dark to shut outer doors."

Some local clergy were later accused of stirring up superstitious fears as part of a sectarian struggle then underway in the region, which had seen some of the affected parishes falling under the sway of an Anglo-Catholic cleric. More sober heads preferred

Above: A line of footprints in the snow; similarly distinctive bipedal prints sparked the Great Devon Mystery.

to look for natural explanations, but mitigating against such were the more extraordinary facts of the case. Ellacombe noted that the creature had made "thousands of these marks . . . on the snow . . . extending over many miles." It was later claimed that the tracks extended across over a hundred miles (160 km), wandering around gardens in some villages, and tracing a single line across countryside, passing unimpeded through impenetrable thickets, along the tops of walls and roofs, through narrow drainpipes and even, supposedly, crossing the River Exe without breaking stride. What kind of animal could produce such singular tracks without regard to the laws of physics?

SPOIL A GOOD STORY

The eminent naturalist Sir Richard Owen, to whom Ellacombe sent drawings of the tracks and even a sample of "white, grape-sized excrement," suggested that badgers were to blame. These animals, while walking, he pointed out, carefully placed their

Below: The River Exe, which proved no bar to the Devil's wanderings.

hindpaws in the prints made by their forepaws, giving their tracks the illusion of being bipedal. Badgers did not have hooves, but perhaps some artifact of thawing and refreezing could account for the apparently uniform shape of the marks. Ellacombe himself suggested birds with ice-encrusted feet. Multiple other culprits were considered (see box on page 135), including donkeys, seagulls, and even migratory eels. But none of these candidates could possibly explain all the strange features of the phenomenon.

What if these weird features were not what they seemed, however? Exeter University research fellow and folklorist Theo Brown later investigated the episode thoroughly, revisiting many of the witnesses' accounts and becoming rather skeptical. She suggested that reports of the trail being continuous and uniform were exaggerated. Probably the tracks appeared over several days, but interviewees preferred not to let the truth get in the way of an exciting fable: "All the people concerned were quite content to leave the thing in the air, rather than spoil a good story." Brown concluded, nonetheless, that "To this day, no one has offered an explanation which takes account of all the available evidence . . . even if the single-footed track only covered a part of the distance we still have no idea what creature could possibly have made it."

OTHER MYSTERY TRACKS

The conventional conclusion is that the mystery of the Devil's Footprints is impossible to solve because of the singular nature of the phenomenon, but in fact there have been similar reports since. Ralph of Coggeshall, a 13th-century chronicler, recorded the appearance of strange hoofprints in the earth after a lightning storm on July 19, 1205; if they were somehow burned into the ground by lightning, it would recall the "branded" nature of the Devil's Footprints. Polar explorer Captain Sir James Clark Ross recorded that a survey party which landed on Kerguelen Island, near the South Pole, in May 1840, reported seeing the tracks of an ass (or donkey) despite the absence of any animals. *The Illustrated*

— FAR OUT —
THEORIES

Above: Could this have been the mystery visitor to fields and gardens across Devon in 1855?

Two of the more prominent theories as to the perpetrator of the Devil's Footprints were an escaped kangaroo and an errant balloon. The former suggestion arose because at the same time as the Footprints flap, it was reported that some kangaroos had escaped from a private zoo belonging to a Mr. Fische at Sidmouth; kangaroos are mainly bipedal, and so the escapees were fingered. In practice, the prints bore no resemblance in size or shape to those of a kangaroo.

Writer Geoffrey Household claimed to have been told by the descendant of a worker at the Devonport Dockyard that an experimental balloon (part of a classified project) had been accidentally released on the night of February 7–8, suggesting that its chain or mooring line had created the tracks as it trailed and bumped along the ground. How this could account for the apparent uniformity of the prints is unclear, and supposedly the prevailing winds would not have pushed the balloon along the correct path either.

London News reported on March 12, 1855, that on the hill of Piaskowa Góra, in Galicia (in modern-day Poland), "every year are to be seen in the snow the same foot-prints as those seen in Devonshire." As recently as March 2009, British newspapers reported marks "in the shape of a cloven hoof" found in a garden in Devon.

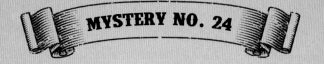
THE THIRD SECRET OF FATIMA

Date: 1917
Location: Fatima, Portugal

An apparition of Mary entrusted three secrets to a shepherd girl, the third of which was hidden in the Vatican archives until 2000; its disclosure failed to satisfy the many who believe that the true secret contains earth-shattering revelations.

The story of the secrets of Fatima is one of prophecy, visions, and conspiracy, which ties together supernatural apparitions, Church politics, papal assassinations, and the Cold War. The story begins in 1917, with a series of visions experienced by a ten-year-old shepherdess, Lúcia dos Santos, and her two companions, Francisco and Jacinta Marto, aged nine and seven, in a pasture near Fatima in Portugal. The three children claimed to have seen a shining lady who told them to return at the same time every month to hear various homilies. Although the apparition, which turned out to be the Blessed Virgin Mary (BVM), swore them to secrecy, word quickly leaked out and despite the skepticism and initial hostility of Church and civic authorities, increasing numbers of people began to accompany the three children. Only the children (and probably only Lúcia) could see the apparition, but others claimed to have seen strange sights.

THE MIRACLE OF THE SUN

The BVM announced that her last visit would be on October 13, and an estimated 70,000 people turned up to witness what became known as the Miracle of the Sun. According to an account by journalist Avelino de Almeida: "the sun . . . looked like a plaque of dull silver and it was possible to look at it without the least discomfort . . . at that moment a great shout went up . . . 'A miracle! A miracle!' . . . the sun trembled, made sudden incredible movements outside all cosmic laws—the sun 'danced' according to the typical expression of the people . . . others . . . swore that the sun whirled on itself like a giant Catherine wheel . . ." The day had been wet and stormy, but the sun supposedly dried out the clothes of the sopping throng with miraculous rapidity.

Skeptics dismiss the "Miracle" as a mix of optical, psychological, and sociological phenomena: a sun dog (an illusion where there appear to be multiple suns), eye movements and retinal distortion, high-altitude cloud screening, and mutually reinforced mass psychogenic delusions. (Significantly, Almeida reports: "People then began to ask each other what they had seen.")

During an earlier apparition, on July 13, the BVM had revealed to Lúcia three secrets. The first was a vision of hell and the

Below: Cousins Jacinta Marto (left) and Lúcia dos Santos, two of the three children to whom the Lady of Fatima appeared.

second a warning that if Russia failed to turn toward the true faith, "she will spread her errors throughout the world, causing wars and persecutions of the Church." These two secrets were revealed to the world in a memoir penned by Lúcia in 1941 (and so can hardly be regarded as genuine prophecies); she also hinted at a third secret, which she did not reveal. Instead, it was sealed in an envelope with instructions that it not be opened until after 1960. In the event, the sealed envelope was passed to the Vatican, and although it was read by some popes and cardinals, it was not revealed to the public until the year 2000.

THE ATTEMPT ON POPE JOHN PAUL II

In the meantime, however, the Third Secret and the Fatima apparitions would play a major role in the drama surrounding the attempted assassination of Pope John Paul II. In St. Peter's Square in Rome on May 13, 1981, the Pope was shot at three times by Mehmet Ali Ağca. The first two shots were fired at his head and would almost certainly have killed him, except that at the crucial moment the pontiff's eye was caught by an image of the Virgin Mary carried by a young girl, and he bent down to hug her. Officially Ağca was a lone gunman, but it is widely accepted that the assassination attempt was coordinated by the Bulgarian secret service, at the behest of the KGB, as part of a plot against a Pope engaged in an anti-Communist crusade. John Paul II was hit in the stomach by the third bullet and his near-death experience led him to have a BVM-related mystical experience of his own. From his hospital room he called for all the material relating to the Fatima visions and read the Third Secret for himself. It apparently confirmed his near-messianic conviction that God had charged him to pursue a sacred battle against Communism.

When the Third Secret was finally published, it proved to relate a vision of "a Bishop dressed in White, [apparently] the Holy Father . . . [when he] reached the top of the mountain, on his knees at the foot of the big Cross, he was killed by a group of soldiers

— FAR OUT —
THEORIES

The man responsible for disseminating the Secret, Cardinal Joseph Ratzinger (later Pope Benedict XVI), recognized that this may not have been the revelation people were expecting, writing that, "the so-called third 'secret' of Fatima, published here in its entirety long after the fact and by decision of the Holy Father, will probably prove disappointing or surprising after all the speculation it has stirred. No great mystery is revealed; nor is the future unveiled." He was right, and today there exists a vigorous subculture both within Catholicism and conspiracy circles, which insists that the Church is suppressing the true Third Secret, or at least refusing to publish

Above: St. Peter's Basilica in the Vatican, Rome; does it still conceal the Third Secret?

all of it. Speculation as to the true content tends to be either apocalyptic or to focus on reactionary criticisms of the Catholic Church, particularly on the "liberalization" introduced by the Second Vatican Council in the 1960s.

who fired bullets and arrows at him." Perhaps understandably John Paul II had related this to his own experience, and the official Catholic line is that the Third Secret was indeed a prophecy of the attempted assassination (but see box).

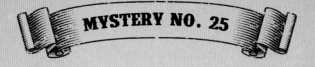
THE LOCH NESS MONSTER

Date: 1933
Location: Loch Ness, Scotland

The world's most famous lake monster can trace her ancestry back at least as far as the 6th century, but Nessie only came to international attention in the 1930s, remaining elusive but captivating ever since.

On September 13, 1933, Mr. and Mrs. McKay were driving down a newly opened road running alongside Scotland's biggest lake, Loch Ness, when they were startled by the appearance of a huge, slimy monster, around 33 feet (10 m) long, with a head and neck like a big snake, which careered across the road and disappeared into the undergrowth. News reports of the encounter kickstarted a media sensation, and the Loch Ness monster was born.

This was not, however, the first time that an aquatic monster had been associated with the Loch Ness region. According to *The Life of Saint Columba* written by St. Adamnan, an Abbot of Iona who died in 704, the Irish abbot and missionary Columba encountered such a beast in 565 CE: "the blessed man was obliged to cross the river Nesa (the Ness); and when he reached the bank of the river,

he saw some of the inhabitants burying an unfortunate man, who . . . was a short time before seized, as he was swimming, and bitten most severely by a monster that lived in the water." Bravely, the "blessed man" ordered someone else to go in the water, but "when the monster felt the water disturbed above by the man swimming, it suddenly rushed out with an awful roar." Undaunted, Columba made the sign of the cross and ordered the beast to "go back with all speed," whereupon "the monster was terrified, and fled more quickly than if it had been pulled back with ropes."

This was not the only marine monster Columba encountered, and Nessie is far from being the only monster to haunt the waterways of the world. Leaving aside the multitudes of sea monsters reported over the centuries, lake monsters have been reported from 250 of the world's lakes and rivers—24 of them in Scotland alone. Following Nessie, many of them have earned sobriquets of their own, including Manipogo, from Lake Manitoba in Canada; Champ, from Lake Champlain on the US–Canadian border; and the Migo of Lake Dakataua in New Britain (although skeptics say this last beast has been wrongly identified from video footage of a man standing up in a canoe).

Above: St. Columbus, using one of his followers to lure out the Loch Ness monster so that he can confront it.

In Sweden, Lake Storsjön is home to a fabled monster, which was the target of a sustained monster-hunting campaign in the 1890s after it was reported to have menaced young girls. Supposedly a company was formed to try to trap the monster; jetties were built, holes cut into the ice, and a Norwegian whaler armed with a harpoon was retained. They even had a giant trap constructed, but to no avail. In 1957 it was claimed that the 19th-century monster hunt had been a tall story fabricated to drum up tourism. Clearly a lake monster is a powerful draw.

Opposite: Loch Ness, a notoriously difficult environment for monster-spotting.

THE SURGEON'S PHOTO

In Scotland, the McKays' tale unleashed a wave of sightings, and photographic evidence was soon to follow. In 1934, army surgeon Lt. Col. Dr. Robert Wilson took what has since become known as the "Surgeon's Photo," a black-and-white picture appearing to show the classic Nessie silhouette of a small head at the end of a serpentine body, rising from just below the surface.

Below: The infamous Surgeon's Photo, actually the work of a group of hoaxers using a toy submarine.

The Surgeon's Photo was later revealed to be a hoax, created by sticking a plastic model onto a toy submarine, but public enthusiasm for Nessie was undaunted. Interest flared up again in 1960 when Tim Dinsdale caught on film a humped object moving across the Loch, apparently at around 7 mph (11 kmh), and this was followed by sonar traces of an unidentified mass off Urquhart Castle, the most productive location for sightings. In the 1970s, underwater cameras produced several sensational images, including what looked like a rhomboidal flipper, and what appeared to be a long-necked, flippered creature. But repeated expeditions to explore, scan, and probe the Loch, together with decades of surface observation, have failed to produce conclusive evidence that Nessie really exists.

One problem is the Loch itself, a unique body of water with features that make it ideal for hiding a large monster. It is 24 miles (38 km) long and 1 mile (1.6 km) wide, and may have underwater connections to the sea. Use of sonar is difficult because of the great depth of the loch (up to 975 ft, or 297 m), the canyons of its deeply ridged floor, and its overhanging sides, which create zones of sonar shadow. Visually scanning the Loch is equally challenging: the surface is frequently misty and the water is thick with particles of peat from the surrounding land, making underwater visibility close to nil. The region is frequently overcast and when the water is in shadow it is notoriously difficult to see below the surface or judge distances accurately.

WITHOUT A TRACE

There are multiple problems with the theory that lake monsters like Nessie are prehistoric survivors (see box on page 145). Firstly, Loch Ness is a cold, freshwater lake, perhaps not the best habitat for a marine reptile that is believed to have been cold-blooded. Even if some species of plesiosaur had survived the extinction that wiped out all its relatives, it would have required a large breeding population to remain viable over millions of years. Loch Ness is too resource-poor to support such a population, although believers argue that submarine tunnels connect the Loch to the open sea—but what about monsters reported from even smaller lakes far from the sea, such as that spotted in Lake Van, high in the mountains of eastern Turkey? More to the point, a considerable population of large creatures, which need to come to the surface to breathe, could surely not remain concealed from legions of monster-hunters. No remains of any such animal have ever been found on the shores of the Loch. Alleged sea-monster carcasses have been recovered from seas and seashores, but all of those that have been investigated have been shown to be the badly decomposed carcasses of non-cryptid animals such as basking sharks. The corpses of large sharks rot in a way that makes them look like a sea serpent, including even hair hanging off the "neck" (shreds of cartilage fiber).

The most likely explanation for lake monster sightings such as Nessie is misidentification of normal animals and other objects, combined with influences from folkloric traditions of monsters. Scotland, for instance, has a long tradition of kelpies: horse-like

— FAR OUT — THEORIES

Far and away the most popular candidate for the identity of Nessie is some species of plesiosaur, a marine reptile from the era of the dinosaurs, which fits many of the classic descriptions. Plesiosaurs had oval bodies with flippers, and long necks with small heads. But there are many other types of water monster reported around the world. Cryptozoologists—those who study conventionally unrecognized creatures—agree that most of them must be prehistoric survivors, ancient species that somehow escaped extinction. Along with plesiosaurs, other candidates include pliosaurs (giant marine reptiles), zeuglodonts (prehistoric whales with sinuous bodies), giant otters, and an unknown species of long-necked seal.

Above: A plesiosaur hauling itself on land; could such a creature have accounted for the McKay sighting of 1933?

fairy creatures that live in lakes. Non-cryptozoological stimuli blamed for monster sightings include misidentified sturgeon, seals, or otters; floating logs, the hulls of upturned boats, or lumps of rotting vegetation, buoyed up by methane; giant conger eels; oarfish or dragonfish (rare types of deep-sea fish that can be many feet or meters long); mini-waterspouts, or rows of leaping porpoises (which could look like a humped monster).

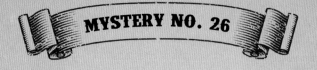
UFOS AND AREA 51

Date: 1947
Location: USA

"Unidentified flying objects" have been widely believed to be extraterrestrial spacecraft, spawning a subculture of conspiracy theories about government cover-ups, secret UFO bases, and alien abductions.

Over 100,000 people have reported a UFO sighting over the last seventy years, and opinion polls reveal that around half of the population in America and other Western countries believe that UFOs are alien spacecraft, with around a quarter convinced that aliens have already made contact (usually implying that governments are covering up this fact). The theory that UFOs are spaceships piloted by aliens from another planet is called the extraterrestrial hypothesis, or ETH.

The UFO phenomenon dates back to June 24, 1947, with the landmark sighting of Kenneth Arnold, a businessman and experienced private pilot. Flying over the Cascade Mountains of Washington State in the northwestern United States, Arnold noticed "a chain of nine peculiar looking aircraft." The vehicles seemed to be moving at a fantastic speed, weaving in and out of the peaks. He observed that they seemed bat-winged or crescent-shaped, and moved like "saucers skipping over water." On landing, Arnold reported his sighting to the military, and the press soon got hold of the story. An anonymous headline writer coined the phrase "flying saucers" and a phenomenon was born. Arnold was a convincing witness, giving careful estimates of the size, distance, and speed of the strange objects, which he interpreted as experimental aircraft. In fact, it seems highly likely that Arnold actually saw a flock of American white pelicans, birds whose profile and flying style correspond exactly to his 1947 description. Within six weeks of Arnold's report, UFO sightings were being reported at the rate of 160 a day.

Above: Kenneth Arnold stands beside his private aircraft, which he was flying when he had his landmark sighting on June 24, 1947, over the Cascade Mountains.

UFOS IN HISTORY

Although ufology is very much a post-World War II phenomenon, researchers soon traced its antecedents much further back. Led by writer Erich von Däniken, a minor industry has grown up around the ancient astronaut hypothesis, in which ancient mysteries are interpreted through the ETH. This places the first encounters with UFOs in prehistoric times, and even posits an extraterrestrial role in creating the human species through genetic engineering.

Historical records have also been mined for relevant encounters. For instance, some medieval chroniclers reported strange encounters with sky ships, similar to conventional ocean-going ones, which let down ladders and interacted with humans. According to Agobard, the 9th-century Bishop of Lyon, many people believed there was a land in the clouds called Magonia, "from which ships, navigating on clouds, set sail." In the late 19th century many newspapers, especially in America, reported waves of sightings of mystery airships—vehicles like dirigibles, but seemingly more advanced, often bearing people dressed in futuristic outfits. Most of the reports were fakes or hoaxes, dreamed up by newspaper editors or local "liars' clubs," where gentlemen would gather to amuse one another with tall tales. During World War II Allied pilots reported many encounters with inexplicable aerial phenomena, even giving them a nickname: "foo fighters." A common feature of UFO reports has always been technology just beyond the capabilities of the day—hence airships in the 19th century and spaceships in the 20th.

Arnold's sighting kicked off what is known as the Golden Age of Ufology. Thousands of people reported daylight disks: flying saucers seen in daylight. The US Air Force opened its own investigation, Project Blue Book, which ended up explaining away most sightings as misidentifications of normal phenomena. Ufologists began to believe the government was engaged in a cover-up, and such suspicions came to focus on one significant event in particular: the 1947 Roswell, New Mexico, incident.

Below: Newsstand dealer Walter McCann supposedly photographed a mystery airship over a Chicago suburb on April 11, 1897; a contemporary artist created this version for a newspaper article.

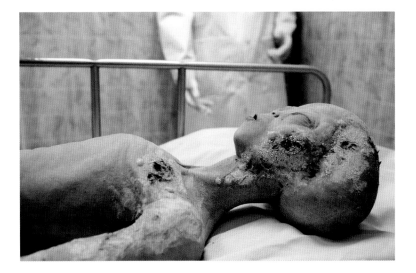

AREA 51

Just two weeks after Arnold's sighting, on July 8, the *Roswell Daily Record* carried an extraordinary headline: "Roswell Army Air Field Captures Flying Saucer on Ranch in Roswell Region." The Air Force was confirming that a flying saucer had crashed the previous week, and its occupants had been taken into custody. But that same afternoon a military press conference announced the "saucer" wreckage was nothing more than a downed weather balloon. The Roswell case later came to assume a central position in the UFO mythology when it was reinvestigated in the 1980s. People who claimed to have worked at Roswell Army Airfield said they had seen autopsies carried out on alien corpses; a film of this later emerged but proved to be a crude hoax.

It was further claimed that the technology recovered from the crash had been spirited away to the top-secret military research base at Area 51. Part of the Groom Lake military testing ground, Area 51 is acknowledged as the research facility where the U2 spyplane and the Stealth Bomber were developed. To ufologists, however, it is also where the recovered alien technology was taken for reverse engineering—the process of working backward from

super-advanced alien technology to arrive at technology that
humans can understand and use—and has since become the site
of a secret alien base, buried beneath the Nevada desert (see box
on page 151). The most likely explanation for the Roswell case
is that it really was a crashed balloon, possibly from a top-secret
high-altitude radar balloon project that was underway at Roswell
in 1947.

THE SKEPTICAL VIEW

Despite the increasingly lurid and baroque developments of
ufology and its attendant conspiracy culture (see box on page
151), nearly 70 years of UFO research have failed to reveal
convincing proof for the ETH. Most UFO sightings can be seen as
simple misidentifications of natural phenomena. Common culprits
include celestial bodies (Venus can be seen during daylight and
is easily perceived as a nearby object moving strangely), birds,
ground-based light sources, aircraft, and atmospheric effects such
as odd clouds or mirages. Photos and videos of flying saucers are
usually revealed as hoaxes or similar misidentifications.

Witness testimony recovered under hypnosis, which forms the
basis of the alien abduction phenomenon, is probably explained
as false memory syndrome, where the interviewer, consciously or
otherwise, suggests a narrative that is then claimed and elaborated
by the subject. There is some evidence that government agencies
such as the CIA or military intelligence made use of ufology as
a means to propagate misinformation about genuine classified
research projects. The theory that the UFO phenomenon can be
explained as anomalous perceptions interpreted through the lens
of cultural and social expectations and narratives is known as
the psychosocial hypothesis (PSH). According to the PSH, UFO
sightings have a psychological origin—such as an hallucination
or misidentification—and are then interpreted by the witness
according to their social and cultural background.

— FAR OUT —
THEORIES

From the 1970s, ufology began to get increasingly weird. Witnesses more frequently reported strange and even supernatural phenomena attending UFO encounters, and a new strain of UFO belief emerged: alien abduction. Under hypnosis, many subjects reported experiencing nighttime visits from aliens, mostly described as having small bodies with large heads and tiny features, except for large oval or tear-drop shaped eyes, often called "grays" from the color of their skin. The classic abductee narrative involves being spirited into a spaceship and then probed or experimented on.

Above: The salt pan of Groom Lake, Nevada—also known as Area 51. Just visible are the runways of the test site, some of the longest in the world.

Some ufologists linked the abductee phenomenon to reports of cattle mutilation, where cows were found with body parts missing, apparently removed with surgical precision, and often associated with sightings of UFOs and black helicopters, believed to be covert government forces. An overarching narrative, sometimes called the Dark Side hypothesis, emerged, claiming that aliens and human governments were engaged in a global conspiracy to create alien-human hybrids, maintain secret alien bases on Earth, and perhaps prepare the planet for colonization or takeover. Area 51 is often pinpointed as the location of one of these bases, concealing a vast underground complex where government agencies collude with the aliens to conduct experiments in genetic manipulation, as well as mind-control technology.

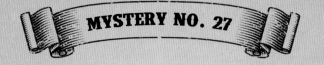
BIGFOOT, SASQUATCH, AND THE YETI

Date: 1950s
Location: Worldwide

Apemen have been reported all over the world, but are particularly well known in America and the Himalayas. But are these reports hoaxes, misidentifications, or evidence of surviving prehistoric hominids?

Apemen are large hairy man-like creatures. The best-known types are Bigfoot and the yeti, but dozens of others have been reported, from Hawaii and New Zealand to Venezuela and Africa. A typical report describes a 10-foot (3-m) high creature with a large head, heavy brows, and long, ape-like arms, which is covered in brown or black fur and often smells repulsive. Some types, such as the *orang pendek* ("little man") of Sumatra, are much smaller than us—around 4 feet (120 cm) high.

Several explorers reported "bushmen" in America in the 18th and 19th centuries, but Bigfoot's story really starts in 1958, when a huge humanoid footprint was found in Humboldt County, Northern California. Probably a hoax, it triggered a national obsession with the creature swiftly christened Bigfoot—also called Sasquatch or Wendigo, after creatures of Native American folklore.

Above: Mountaineers catch a glimpse of the Abominable Snowman in the Himalayas, in this drawing from the 1950s.

It is estimated that over a thousand Americans claim to have seen Bigfoot, with most reports coming from states in the northwest. Obviously this region has the most forested wilderness, but Bigfoot apparently refuses to be bound by biogeographical common sense, insisting on appearing in practically every state in America. A well-known example is the Florida skunk ape, which gets its name from the terrible smell reported by witnesses. One of the most famous Bigfoot encounters is that of Albert Ostman, who claimed to have been kidnapped by a family of Sasquatch in 1924. He managed to escape by feeding snuff to one of them, causing a sneezing fit. Some Bigfoot witnesses even claim to have shot one, but hard evidence remains frustratingly hard to come by, despite finds such as hair, droppings, and even alleged Bigfoot fingerprints.

THE ABOMINABLE SNOWMAN

Reports of apemen in the Himalayas date back at least as far as the 14th century, but the yeti only really hit the headlines in 1921 when a British explorer, Lieutenant-Colonel C. K. Howard-Bury, spotted some strange creatures on a distant snowfield in the

Everest region. When he discovered huge footprints at the same spot, his porters told him they belonged to a strange creature—the *metoh-kangmi*. This was later erroneously translated by a reporter as "Abominable Snowman." The Himalayan apeman has since become known as the yeti, which according to one translation simply means "that-there thing."

Eric Shipton's 1951 photographs of an 18-inch (33-cm) footprint and the 1960 expedition of Sir Edmund Hillary (conqueror of Everest) stirred public interest in the yeti to fever pitch, especially when Hillary brought back a skullcap purported to be made of yeti hide. It turned out to be goatskin. In one of the stranger incidents in cryptozoology, Hollywood actor James Stewart had smuggled a supposed yeti finger out of Nepal in 1959. It turned out to be a mummified human finger. Definitive proof of the yeti's existence is yet to be discovered and there have been few recent sightings.

Below: This iconic photograph of a mysterious footprint in the Himalayan snow was taken by British Everest mountaineer Eric Shipton in 1951, on one of the Menlung basin glaciers.

MAN IN A MONKEY SUIT

The best evidence for Bigfoot is probably the 1967 Patterson–Gimlin film, supposedly showing a female specimen ambling across a clearing in Bluff Creek, California. While many people claim that this is simply a man in a monkey suit, it has never been conclusively proved to be a hoax. Some experts claim that the springy gait of the creature in the film could not have been faked—others disagree.

Skeptics claim that apeman sightings can be explained as hoaxes or misidentifications. Sightings of bears rearing up on their hind legs probably

— FAR OUT —
THEORIES

Above: The cave on Flores island in Indonesia where remains were found that researchers claimed belonged to a new species of human.

According to conventional scientific thinking, modern humans (*Homo sapiens*) are the only surviving members of the hominid family, which in the past included *Homo erectus* and the Neanderthals. The discovery in 2003 of remains on the Indonesian island of Flores, attributed, albeit controversially, to an extinct hominid labeled *Homo floresiensis* (aka the hobbit) galvanized a school of thought in cryptozoology that identifies apemen as relic hominids. As with the sea serpent or Loch Ness Monster (see page 140), apemen may be prehistoric survivors, managing to survive undetected in wilderness areas.

Bigfoot and the yeti, for example, could theoretically be surviving examples of *Gigantopithecus*, a relative of early man thought to have died out 300,000 years ago, while descriptions of the alma, an apeman reported from Mongolia, closely resemble Neanderthal man, *Homo neanderthalensis*, thought to have become extinct 30,000 years ago. The *orang pendek* of Sumatra could potentially be a surviving form of *Homo erectus*, the first hominid species to have left Africa and settled across the globe, or perhaps a surviving population of *Homo floresiensis*.

account for many of the sightings, and one explanation for footprints in the snow is that prints left by small animals (such as rabbits) melt together in the sun to form larger marks.

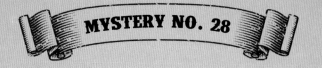

THE WOW! SIGNAL FROM OUTER SPACE

Date: 1977

Location: Constellation Sagittarius, about 2.5 degrees south of Chi Sagittarii, near the M55 globular cluster

In 1977, a radio telescope searching the skies for broadcasts from extraterrestrial civilizations picked up a very strong signal, highlighted on a printout with the comment "Wow!" The nature and source of this signal remain a mystery today.

Described by *National Geographic* as "both the first and best potential evidence of communication from extraterrestrials, and one of the most perplexing mysteries in science," the Wow! signal was picked up by Ohio State University's now-defunct Big Ear radio observatory at 11:16pm Eastern Daylight Time on August 15, 1977. Nobody noticed anything strange about Big Ear's recordings until a few days later, when volunteer astronomer Jerry Ehman, part of the Search for Extraterrestrial Intelligent Life (SETI) project, was analyzing the output from the computer printer. The way the system worked was that the radio telescope picked up radio signals with its antennae and fed them into an IBM 1130 mainframe computer, which measured the strength of the signal on a 35-point scale, with scores higher than 9 being given the letters of the alphabet. These scores

Above: The Ohio State University Radio Observatory, known as the Big Ear, which was located in Delaware, Ohio.

were printed out onto graph paper, which had to be laboriously analyzed, by eye, by a human volunteer.

THE MOST SIGNIFICANT THING

Working through the long stretches of zeros, 1s, and 2s that represent the background hiss of the cosmos, Ehman was startled to see a sequence of scores that climbed from 6, to E, all the way up to U (30 points higher than the background hiss), before subsiding back down to 5, so that the whole sequence read 6EQUJ5. Plotted on a graph, this shows a spike in radio signal intensity that stands out from the background noise like a red flag against a white background. It was exactly what SETI had been looking for. "Without thinking, I wrote 'Wow!'" Ehman recalls. "It was the most significant thing we had seen."

This string of six alphanumeric values is potentially the most significant discovery in the history of the human race. To understand why, it is necessary to learn more about the search for life in the universe. In the early 1960s, Cornell physicists Philip Morrison and Giuseppe Cocconi had developed the theory behind what became SETI. They reasoned that the best evidence to look for in the search for intelligent life would be radio signals, as it takes relatively little energy for these to travel far across the universe. At the time, one of the few natural emission frequencies known was that of hydrogen gas, which, when it changes energy state, emits radio waves at the frequency 1420 megahertz. Radio telescopes around the world were already looking at this frequency, and Morrison and Cocconi figured that extraterrestrial civilizations, aware of the same natural phenomenon, would use this as the frequency on which to broadcast their own "We are here" signal.

BROADCAST FROM ANOTHER WORLD

The Wow! signal was broadcasting on precisely this frequency, and it was loud. If the signal were coming from a distant transmitter and shooting across the universe in a beam, then as the Big Ear telescope, fixed to the Earth, rotated through that beam, the signal would be expected to grow in intensity to a peak and then drop off again as the telescope passed through the beam and out the other side. This is precisely what the 6EQUJ5 signal shows. Big Ear was listening on 50 channels at once, and the Wow! signal appeared on just one of those channels. According to astronomer Robert Gray, one of the leading experts on the Wow! signal, "that's just not the way natural radio sources work. Natural radio sources diffuse static across all frequencies, rather than hitting at a single frequency. So it's pretty clear that this was a radio signal and not a quasar or pulsar or some other natural radio source, of which there are millions. It was very narrow band, very concentrated, exactly like a radio station, or a broadcast, from another world would look."

Unfortunately, the excitement generated by the extraordinary signal dissipated when it proved impossible to detect again. The

— FAR OUT —
THEORIES

Above: The Hat Creek Allen Telescope Array, radio telescopes used by SETI.

If the Wow! signal was not an alien broadcast, what was it? The profile of the signal made it unlikely to have been a terrestrial source or interference, while civilian satellites are not allowed to broadcast on that frequency. Secret military transmitters would be foolish to broadcast on a frequency that the world's astronomers are scanning, and if the signal had come from a satellite it would likely have recurred. Ehman considered the possibility that it was a terrestrial signal reflected from space junk but now discounts this, describing the nature of the Wow! signal as "an open question." Skeptics point out that a data set consisting of six values is a weak basis on which to construct grand theories about the existence of alien civilizations, and Ehman himself cautions, "I refuse to draw vast conclusions from half-vast data."

Big Ear telescope never found the signal again, and it never heard anything as loud. Numerous other searches, including some by the world's largest radio telescope arrays, have failed to find the Wow! signal. Pinpointing its apparent original location proved difficult because the Big Ear telescope scanned a relatively large portion of the sky, but the signal appeared to be coming from somewhere in the constellation Sagittarius, about 2.5 degrees south of the star Chi Sagittarii, near the M55 globular cluster.

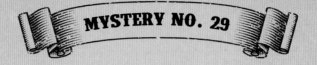
WEEPING AND BLEEDING STATUES

Date: 1970s
Location: Worldwide

Statues that weep, bleed, drink milk, or display other miraculous behaviors are known from around the world and throughout history. But are they pious frauds or divine interventions?

Religious mysteries constitute an entire category of their own. An appetite for incursions of the supernatural world into the natural one seems to be a very ancient urge. In the Classical era statues regularly wept, among other prodigious feats, abilities linked to the widespread belief that gods and spirits could readily inhabit the statues made in their honor. One particularly notable example was the statue of Apollo at Cumae. The ancient writer Julius Obsequens records that in 130 BCE, "A statue of Apollo wept for four days," which the early Christian philosopher Augustine later adduced as evidence that the demonic pagan gods were already mourning their coming demise well in advance of the arrival of Jesus. The Classical era had its skeptics and mythbusters, though; for instance, Cicero attempted to rationalize the wetness of sweating statues as nothing more than condensation.

Right: A statue of the Blessed Virgin Mary weeping, or at least with some liquid on its face.

WEEPING ICONS

The spread of Christianity in the Roman Empire, with its prohibitions on idol worship, might have been expected to put a stop to the antics of statues, especially religious ones, but in fact Christian images and statues proved to be just as active as pagan ones. In the 6th century, St. Gregory of Tours reported that weeping statues were being used to win converts to Christianity, while medieval pilgrims to the Holy Land reported weeping icons. The habit spread into Europe. The Austrian emperor Leopold I acquired from Marijapovch, in north-eastern Hungary, a Madonna and Child icon that began weeping in 1715; it was itself a copy of an icon that had been weeping for ten years. An even earlier icon, from Klokochovo in Slovakia, had been weeping since 1670.

Bleeding was another favorite stunt for religious images. One famous account concerns a "miraculous painting" of the Virgin Mary of Mantua, in northern Italy, which was stolen in the 17th century and used by early gun nuts for target practice. When struck by a bullet it began to bleed from its wound, and it is said that the painting (now kept in Prague) still bleeds to this day.

WAVE OF WEEPERS

The modern wave of weeping statues began in earnest in the 1970s and '80s, with the vast majority concerning statues of the Blessed Virgin Mary (BVM). The BVM has a long history in Catholicism of featuring in apparitions and visions (see The Third Secret of Fatima, page 136), and is often described shedding a tear for the sins of humanity and the awful fate that awaits the world if sinners fail to repent and return to the correct path of religion. Similar motives are attributed to weeping statues of the BVM, and also to the less popular weeping Jesus statues. Countries that have reported weeping BVM or Jesus statues since the 1970s include Australia, Bangladesh, Benin, Bolivia, Canada, Ecuador, Haiti, Ireland, Italy (with eight post-1970 incidents), Japan, Mexico, Philippines, Puerto Rico, Romania, Russia, Spain, Syria (1977), Trinidad, USA (with at least 15 post-1970 reports), and Venezuela. A similar list of countries have reported bleeding statues.

Weeping BVMs often shed tears of oil rather than salty water, placing their exudates in a long tradition of holy oil. According to the faithful, this oil is of divine provenance, but on occasions when samples have been collected and tested, they generally prove to be olive oil or other vegetable oils. The blood shed by statues has also been analyzed on numerous occasions. In those cases where it has proven to be human blood, the faithful claim that it is the blood of Mary or Jesus, respectively, although it is notable that when gender can be determined it often matches that of the owner of the statue, not the statue.

PIOUS FRAUDS

The skeptical point of view is that active statues are all forms of fraud, although many may be pious frauds, which is where they are perpetrated by the faithful, either unconsciously or in order to serve a pious end (such as reinforcing the faith and making converts). In most cases tears, oil, and blood are probably applied by hand, but Italian skeptic Luigi Garlaschelli famously proposed

— FAR OUT —
THEORIES

Some findings have led to creative interpretations. Blood from a bleeding Virgin Mary statue belonging to noted stigmatic Sister Agnes Sasagawa of Akita, in Japan, in 1973, was found to contain three different blood types; a bishop suggested it was blood from all three members of the Trinity, although he did not record the likely reaction of God and the Holy Spirit to the discovery that they had corporeal forms.

In another case, blood from a statue of Jesus was found to be female, prompting documentary-maker Michael Willesee to claim that this was only to be expected given Jesus's virgin birth, which meant that he only had a female parent.

Above: A statue of the Virgin Mary, known as Our Lady of Akita.

a simple mechanism: "What is needed is a hollow statue made of a porous material such as plaster or ceramic . . . glazed or painted with some sort of impermeable coating . . . [and] filled up with a liquid . . . If the glazing is imperceptibly scratched . . . around the eyes, tear-like drops will leak out . . . this trick proved to be very satisfactory, baffling all onlookers."

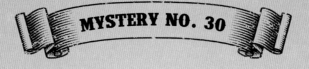

PHANTOM BIG CATS

Date: 1960s
Location: Britain, Europe, America, Australia

Out-of-place big cats have been spotted with amazing frequency in the British Isles and beyond since the 1960s, yet the official line is there are no feral big cats in Britain. Experts remain furiously divided on the issue.

They are variously known as phantom big cats, out-of-place animals, mystery cats, or, to those most involved in the field, alien (in the sense of non-native) big cats, or ABCs. The phenomenon's epicenter is in Britain, but ABCs have been reported in most of Europe, Australia, and parts of America where big cats are no longer believed to be present in the wild.

A typical ABC report describes a panther-like feline, usually around the size of a large labrador, with black fur, although tawny fur is also fairly common. As a result, such creatures are usually reported as panthers or pumas. Occasionally, reports speak of creatures resembling a lynx or a lion without a mane (a female), but there are few, if any, reports of big cats with spots, stripes, or manes. The prevalence and frequency of these reports is very high, especially in Britain. Between April 2004 and July 2005, for instance, the British Big Cat Society recorded 2,123 big cat sightings. As well as sightings, farmers often report livestock depredations that appear not to match typical patterns of killing by wild predators or stray dogs, particularly noting so-called "clean kills" where elements such as fur removal and bites to the neck seem to match big cat habits. In addition, there have been many identifications of tracks and spoor said to belong to big cats.

MOOR BEASTS

The ABC as a media phenomenon dates back to the flap around the Surrey Puma in the 1960s. This was a large, tawny feline seen in the English county of Surrey by numerous witnesses, described as resembling a puma (also known as a mountain lion, or cougar). Despite extensive searches and continued witness sightings into the 1970s, the Surrey Puma was never tracked down. In 1983, a new ABC came on the scene: the Beast of Exmoor, mainly identified as a black panther but also linked to reports of creatures resembling

Below: A map showing all of the big cat sightings in just the small county of Cambridgeshire, England, since 1982.

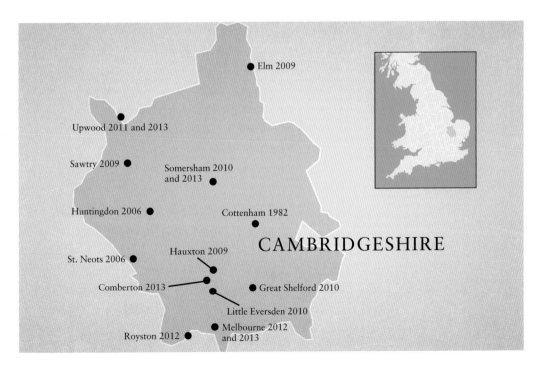

Elm 2009

Upwood 2011 and 2013

Sawtry 2009

Somersham 2010 and 2013

Huntingdon 2006

Cottenham 1982

CAMBRIDGESHIRE

Hauxton 2009

St. Neots 2006

Comberton 2013

Great Shelford 2010

Little Eversden 2010

Melbourne 2012 and 2013

Royston 2012

a puma and a lynx. Many other British ABCs followed, including the Dartmoor Beast and, most infamously, the Beast of Bodmin Moor, the focus of a 1995 government investigation.

Believers in ABCs generally point to the introduction in Britain of the Dangerous Wild Animals (DWA) Act in 1976. This meant that it was now mandatory to get a license for keeping a big cat as a pet, which in turn meant a great deal of effort and expense. It is possible that many owners decided surreptitiously to turn their now illegal pets loose into the wild, providing an obvious source for a small population of feral ABCs. Another theory is that ABCs have hybridized with each other or domestic cats to create a viable long-term feral population of large wild cats.

THE CASE AGAINST

Skeptics point to a host of problems with these theories. Firstly, big cats such as pumas generally don't live more than 15 years, so sustaining a feral population after 1991 would require a fairly large number of animals with lairs and territories. Secondly, there is the notorious difficulty of judging scale and distance for even the most apparently capable witnesses. The official study into the Beast of Bodmin, for instance, concluded that the animals reported were actually normal-sized domestic cats. Thirdly, skeptics dispute the hybridization theory, pointing out that panther family big cats only cross-mate if reared together, while hybrids produced with domestic cats would be neither fertile nor particularly large.

Fourth is the issue of melanism; the majority of ABC reports are of black (melanistic) animals, yet melanism of leopards and jaguars is incredibly rare, and is not known in pumas. If ABCs are released leopards and pumas (jaguars are not kept as pets), why are so many of them melanistic? Lastly, and seemingly most damningly, skeptics say that there is no hard evidence in the form of dead animals, live captures, and unambiguous spoor and trails.

— FAR OUT —
THEORIES

One of the problems facing ABC researchers is that little is straightforward in the field. A typical media flap involves witness reports, followed by fruitless searches by police and animal control, followed by further reports until eventually the flap dies down with no clear resolution. In addition, ABC reports are often not restricted to straightforward sightings of real-world animals, but include weird and paranormal elements such as eerie sensations, UFO sightings, ghostly disappearances, and unnatural characteristics (such as flaming eyes). On top of this, elements of the ABC community have developed conspiracy theories accusing the authorities of suppressing the truth about phantom cats for dark ends.

Above: European wildcats may be responsible for some ABC sightings.

But not all of these objections are well-founded. In fact, there is a surprising amount of hard evidence for ABCs, with many dead specimens—at least one Eurasian lynx, and several smaller felines such as jungle cats and leopard cats—and a living puma and lynx having been captured. Black panthers, however, remain elusive.

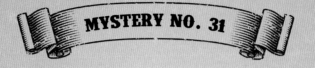

CROP CIRCLES

Date: 1970s
Location: Wiltshire, England

Patterns in fields of crops have appeared frequently since the 1970s, but are they landscape art, clever hoaxes, messages from aliens, or evidence of unknown natural forces?

The modern crop circle phenomenon is usually traced back to Queensland, Australia, in 1966. Small, rough circles of flattened plants appeared, which local UFO investigators nicknamed "saucer nests." Some people claimed to have seen UFOs rising above them. But these early circles may have even older antecedents, in the work of a destructive Mowing Devil. This engaging imp was identified in a 1678 woodcut pamphlet, published in England, and titled *The Mowing-Devil: or, Strange News out of Hartford-shire*. The pamphlet told of a farmer who rashly declared, on refusing to pay the fee demanded by a laborer, that he would rather the Devil mowed his field instead. Mysterious flames appeared in the field overnight, and the next day the crop had been "so neatly mow'd by the Devil or some Infernal Spirit, that no Mortal Man was able to do the like." What is particularly striking for modern crop circle researchers is that the woodcut illustration, which shows a devil hard at work with a scythe, depicts the crops being cut in concentric circles, clearly suggesting supernatural agency had been ascribed to an early example of the crop circle phenomenon.

UNDER THE WHITE HORSE

The first crop circles started to appear in fields in southern England in 1975, but they were not picked up by the media until 1980. That same year a pattern of three circles appeared, and each successive summer saw the appearance of increasingly complex and intricate patterns. Most of the circles appeared within a relatively small area: Alton, in Wiltshire, England, near the Alton Barnes white horse. Normally crop circles appear overnight, but some people claimed to have seen them form. Crop circle patterns now include rings, symbols, lattices of straight and curved lines, and even complex mathematically generated fractal shapes.

Below: A crop circle in a corn field below Pewsey Downs near Avebury, Wiltshire, in England.

A NEW CROP OF TRIBES

The growing enthusiasm for crop circles engendered new cultural tribes. Circle makers claimed to be the ones creating the circles, usually as a kind of landscape art experiment. Cropwatchers or "croppies" kept watch for crop circles forming, hung out in local pubs, and were often suspected of close links to circle makers. Cereologists (also spelled cerealogists) tried to study the phenomenon scientifically, hoping to identify previously unknown natural phenomena at work, although many also used fringe science and New Age techniques such as dowsing. All three of these groups have reported strange phenomena associated with crop circles, including earth lights (mystery lights that seem to be linked to geology—see box on page 175), tingling sensations and shocks big enough to knock people over, healing powers, and UFO and ghost sightings.

STALK-STOMPERS

In 1991, a pair of artists and UFO enthusiasts from Southampton, Doug Bower and Dave Chorley, claimed they had created all the initial circles as a joke. They admitted to hoaxing approximately 250 circles over the years, having been inspired by the Queensland saucer nests of the 1960s. They claimed to use just their feet, and later a plank of wood with a rope attachment, known as a "stalk-stomper," to make the circles. It soon became apparent that there were other circle-making groups, with names like the Bill Bailey Gang, Merlin and Co, and Spiderman and Catwoman. Their motives were mischievous and artistic. Between them, the circle makers claimed responsibility for nearly every single circle.

It now seems likely that almost all crop circles are man-made, but some mysteries still remain. Who or what created the original saucer nests? Why do man-made circles seem to produce paranormal phenomena? Why do so many people continue to insist that most crop circles are not man-made?

— FAR OUT —
THEORIES

Above: A crop circle in Diessenhofen, Switzerland, viewed from the air.

A significant number of croppies and cereologists reject the claims of the hoaxers. When crop circles first appeared, one of the initial theories to gain support was that UFOs are creating the circles, either when landing or taking off, or as some kind of message to mankind. Skeptics point out that crop glyphs make for a "low-bandwidth" medium. Meteorologist Dr. Terence Meaden, who became a leading cereologist, initially suggested that the circles were made by small whirlwinds, or dust devils, formed by the wind eddying round the sides of hills. As the formations became more complex, Meaden elaborated his theory.

Perhaps the small whirlwinds generated their own electric charge, becoming "plasma vortices" (tiny tornadoes of hot, electrically charged gas). Meaden claimed that such vortices could leave complex patterns of spirals and rings. Meaden's theory received dramatic support in 1991 when a couple claimed to have been in the middle of a circle as it was created. They heard a high-pitched whine, and were pressed to the ground by a powerful wind as their hair stood on end—exactly as Meaden's theory predicted. By now, though, patterns involving complex symbols were appearing. Clearly, some sort of intelligence was behind the crop circles. For true believers, aliens were back in the frame, or perhaps some kind of natural or cosmic intelligence.

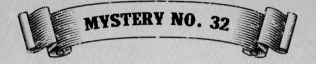
GHOST OR SPIRIT ORBS

Date: 1990s
Location: Worldwide

Blobs, spots, and circles of light visible in photographs are emanations of the spirit world, according to believers—although skeptics have far more mundane explanations.

Orbs, also known as balls of light (BOLs), have been hailed by many in the ghost-hunting and spiritualist community as proof of life after death, unknown energy phenomena, and the existence of ghosts. A typical orb is a bright spot of light caught on a photograph, not visible with the naked eye when the photo was taken. Orbs vary greatly in size and composition. Variants on the orb include similar but less circular shapes labeled rods, "light slugs," and vortices. They are particularly commonly found at popular ghost-hunting sites such as haunted houses.

Some believers suggest that the orb is the "energy signature" of a paranormal phenomenon, such as a haunting. Others claim to see faces or messages in orbs, which supports claims that they are discarnate spirits or media for communication with such spirits.

The orb phenomenon properly kicked off with the advent of widely available digital photography in the 1990s. This coincided with the emergence of the internet as a global forum, and hence the orb meme propagated and thrived in cyberspace. A whole subculture of orb photography and belief emerged, and there have even been courses offered in orb photography.

Above: Orbs captured on film at Harpers Ferry Cemetery, West Virginia, in the USA.

DUST TO DUST

To skeptics, the popularity and—to an even greater extent—the endurance of this meme is baffling, because orbs are one of the most easily debunked of paranormal phenomena, probably rating as the least mysterious topic covered in this book. It has been convincingly demonstrated over and over again that orbs are artifacts of photography, created when light—usually from a flash—reflects off particles in the atmosphere, bounces off objects such as camera straps, is reflected within camera lenses, or some combination of all of these.

The first explanation is probably the most common: the air is full of particles of dust, spores, insects, tiny droplets of water, and myriad other types. As digital cameras became popular and accessible, they usually took the form of compact cameras, where the flash is close to the lens. Apart from causing the well-known phenomenon of red eye, this also heightens the chances of catching on camera artifacts of flash usage. The sites where ghost-hunters most assiduously seek orbs are just those where large amounts of atmospheric debris are common, such as dusty old houses or damp graveyards. Anyone can readily capture orbs on camera for themselves by taking a flash picture on a rainy night or in a dusty room. To produce an orb, the reflective particle usually needs to be close to the lens, which accounts for the fact that orbs are rarely seen obscured by or emerging from behind background objects; they are caused by minute specks in the foreground.

WILD ENTHUSIASMS

Given the ease and regularity with which the orb phenomenon has been debunked, perhaps the true mystery of orbs is why so many people still believe they are paranormal. The answer lies in human psychology, and was articulated at least as early as 1875, when medium William Stainton Moses, commenting on people's gullibility when it came to so-called spirit photographs, noted: "Some people would recognize anything [as a ghost]. A broom and a sheet are quite enough for some wild enthusiasts who go with the figure in their eye and see what they wish to see . . . I have had pictures that might be anything in this or any other world sent to me and gravely claimed as recognized portraits." The will to believe has often proven to be insurmountable by evidence or rational argument. The same year that Moses decried "wild enthusiasts," infamous spirit photographer Jean Buguet was convicted of fraud after confessing and having his stock of fake heads displayed in court. Nonetheless, many of those duped by him continued to insist not only that he was genuine but so were the photographs he had faked.

—FAR OUT—
THEORIES

Orbs visible to the naked eye have been linked to a related phenomenon known as earth lights. These are usually points or balls of light, seen moving with no apparent cause or origin, and often associated with particular spots, as with the Hessdalen lights in Norway or the Longendale lights in Derbyshire, England. One theory is that they are forms of ball lightning—spheres of plasma (ionized gas) created by piezoelectric effects (where pressure generates an electrical current) on quartz crystalline rock, which is under pressure at geological faults or boundaries. Also known as "spook lights" and "ghost lights," earth lights can vary in color and shape, and have been reported making sounds, leaving trails, and even exploding (all phenomena seen with ball lightning). Some people insist that there is some form of intelligence behind earth lights, which appear to interact with observers.

Above: *Will o' the Wisp*, by Arnold Böcklin, 1862; also known as *ignis fatuus* ("foolish fire") or marsh lights, this phenomenon may be related to similarly described earth lights.

CRYPTIC ARTIFACTS

This chapter investigates seven extraordinary objects of two types: those that allegedly possess incredible powers, and those that confound the archaeological record and resist conventional explanation. What connects them all is the possibility that they represent technology that is out of time, and which thus threatens to overturn traditional understanding of history.

The Fuente Magna bowl is a large stone dish, allegedly discovered from an ancient pre-Columbian site in Bolivia, which appears to bear inscriptions in writing similar to the cuneiform of ancient Mesopotamia. If it is real—which is extremely doubtful—it seems to

back up the contention of transatlantic cultural exchange long before Columbus sailed the ocean blue. Also resisting decipherment are the inscriptions on the Phaistos Disk—a clay tablet from an ancient Minoan site printed with strange hieroglyphs, thousands of years before printing was thought to have been invented—and in the Voynich Manuscript, a medieval book of weird and wonderful illustrations. The Baghdad Battery is one of many ancient Persian jars that resemble battery technology, over a millennium before its time, while the Antikythera Mechanism is an ancient Greek astronomical computer of dazzling ingenuity. The Turin Shroud and the Ark of the Covenant, meanwhile, are both artifacts of awesome religious significance.

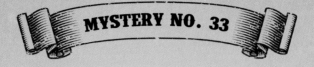

THE FUENTE MAGNA BOWL

Date: Either *ca.* 2500 BCE or *ca.* 1958 CE
Location: La Paz, Bolivia

A large bowl, allegedly discovered near Lake Titicaca in Bolivia, is said to bear ancient Old World writing, suggesting transatlantic links at least 4,000 years before Columbus.

The Fuente Magna bowl is a large dish or bowl, apparently made out of an earthen-reddish stone, engraved with drawings of human and animal motifs and marks said to resemble cuneiform writing. The Spanish word *fuente* can mean "bowl" or "source," and "Fuente Magna" has been described as the location where the bowl was found, although a more plausible explanation is simply that it means "Big Bowl."

The main source for information on the Fuente Magna is an online article, apparently translated from Spanish and since disseminated widely across the web, by two independent investigators from Bolivia: Bernardo Biados and Freddy Arce. They claim the bowl was first discovered by accident at the Chua Hacienda near Lake Titicaca, about 47 miles (75 km) from La Paz, and that it came to the attention of a Bolivian archaeologist, Don Max Portugal

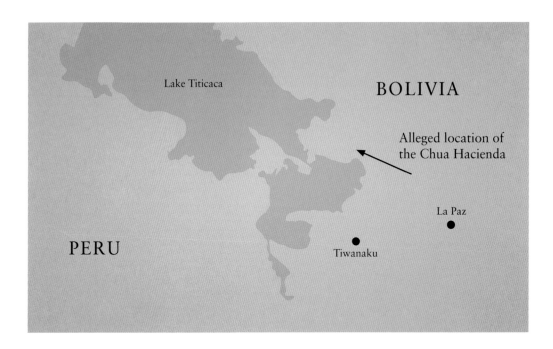

Lake Titicaca

BOLIVIA

Alleged location of
the Chua Hacienda

La Paz

PERU

Tiwanaku

around 1958. Don Portugal "rescued" the bowl and attempted repairs upon it, but it was not until the late 1970s that it was suggested that the marks on the bowl were cuneiform writing.

Above: A map of Lake Titicaca and the surrounding area, showing the crucial locations in the story of the bowl's discovery.

THE POKOTIA MONOLITH

Around 2000, Biados and Arce visited La Paz's Museo de Metales Preciosos, aka the Museum of Gold, where the bowl now resides, and tried to follow up the account of the dish's recovery. Traveling to the presumed location of Chua, they tracked down a 98-year-old man named Maximiliano, who recognized a photo of the Fuenta Magna as a bowl he had once used as a dish for pig feed, many decades previously. Maximiliano directed them to the site from which, he claimed, it had been found, which turned out to be an area of mounds that might be the remains of stepped ziggurats. This area is close to the ruins of the ancient civilization of Tiwanaku. Biados and Arce also claim to have discovered, in 2002, a 6.5-foot (2-m) high monolithic idol, which they call the Pokotia Monolith, also bearing cuneiform-like inscriptions.

The apparent significance of the Fuente Magna bowl is that the marks on it have been identified as a variety of ancient Old World writing systems. Dr. Alberto Marini first suggested the marks were cuneiform writing in an ancient Sumerian style. More recently, the marks have been identified by American anthropologist Hugh Bernard Fox as ancient Phoenician writing, while Biados and Arce sent photos of the bowl to Dr. Clyde Winters, who identified it as proto-Sumerian cuneiform, dating back to *ca.* 3000 BCE. Winters even translated the inscription, which begins, "Girls take an oath to act justly [this] place. [This is] a favorable oracle of the people. Send forth a just divine decree. The charm [the Fuente Magna] [is] full of Good." Winters's translation suggests the inscriptions concern the ritual use of the dish, which was probably to pour libations—offerings to a deity or idol, perhaps the very Pokotia Monolith that Biados and Arce discovered.

Above: Genuine cuneiform writing from an ancient Mesopotamian tablet.

Opposite: A reed boat on Lake Titicaca; similarities have been drawn between such vessels and ancient Egyptian reed boats.

THE ROSETTA STONE OF THE AMERICAS

If any of these identifications are accurate, this artifact would be the single greatest archaeological discovery in the Americas—perhaps of all time. Indeed, Biados and Arce call the bowl "the Rosetta Stone of the Americas." In mainstream chronology, the first contact between New and Old World civilizations, outside of the far north of North America, came in 1492 when Columbus "sailed the ocean blue." But there is a thriving subculture in fringe archaeology and alternative or pseudo-history, which investigates evidence that transatlantic contacts go back much further. Winters, for instance, is a firm believer in very ancient or even prehistoric links between the Old and New Worlds, while Fox argues that the precious metal mines of Bolivia correspond to biblical locations such as Tarshish or Ophir, with which King Solomon traded.

There are several other New World artifacts said to bear cuneiform inscriptions, while other evidence includes the supposed presence of coca residues in ancient Egyptian mummies, Phoenician coins apparently discovered in the Americas, similarities between the

iconography of ancient South American pottery and ancient Greek art, and a variety of cultural similarities between Old and New World civilizations, such as measurement units, monumental architecture, funeral rites, and even boatbuilding. In fact, the supposed similarities between reed boats constructed by ancient Egyptians on the Nile and those still built on Lake Titicaca suggest an obvious mode of transport by which transatlantic communication was effected. The seaworthiness of ocean-going reed boats and the plausibility of transatlantic crossings in them was dramatically demonstrated by Norwegian adventurer Thor Heyerdahl in his Ra expeditions of 1969 and 1970.

One suggestion is that the Fuente Magna inscriptions back up an earlier theory that Aymara, the language spoken by the indigenous peoples of Bolivia's Altiplano region, is related to ancient Sumerian (both are what are known as agglutinative languages). South American words such as "Inca" may thus actually be related to Sumerian terms such as "Enki" (the name of a major Sumerian deity, meaning "great lord").

BAD CUNEIFORM

Mainstream archaeology has taken little notice of the Fuente Magna bowl. It is generally dismissed as a fake. Archaeologist Keith Fitzpatrick-Matthews, who runs the "Bad Archaeology" blog, points out sources for the Fuente Magna bowl are generally recycled versions of the same translated article, and that even this account makes clear the provenance of the artifact is suspect at best. The earliest evidence of the bowl is in 1958, and there is no record of the site mentioned as its origin or its discoverers. Biados and Arce's provenance for the bowl seems to rest on recollections from a barely identified 98-year-old man. As for the markings, while they may resemble cuneiform, Fitzpatrick-Matthews points out that they don't resemble it that much, but do look like someone ineptly trying to copy cuneiform. They are evidently indistinct enough to support at least three different interpretations

— FAR OUT —
THEORIES

Above: Ignatius Donnelly, one-time US Congressman and alternative history author.

The real agenda behind many "alternative" historical claims made about the Fuente Magna bowl is to support the case for an Atlantean origin (with roots in the legendary island empire of Atlantis—see page 10) for ancient Indo-American civilizations, and for the common-origin account of supposed similarities between Old and New World civilizations. Lake Titicaca, for instance, sits at the epicenter of an unlikely but vigorous school of thought placing Atlantis on the Bolivian altiplano, while Ignatius Donnelly, the godfather of modern Atlantean studies, leaned heavily on similarities between the Old and New Worlds—such as sun-worship and pyramids—as a keystone of his argument that ancient civilizations shared a common origin in Atlantis. There is also a darker side to theories of pre-Columbian transatlantic contact, which can be abused by those who wish to argue that Native American claims to the New World would be superseded if it could be proven that Old World cultures settled there first and founded the great New World civilizations.

(Sumerian, proto-Sumerian, and Phoenician) by three different historians. The rest of the iconography on the bowl is said to match that of the Tiwanaku culture, which dates to around 100–1000 CE, some 3,000 years after ancient Sumeria.

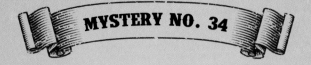

THE PHAISTOS DISK

Date: *ca.* 1700 BCE
Location: Phaistos, southern Crete

An engimatic clay disk, block printed with hieroglyphs in an indecipherable, unknown script, is unique in the ancient world—and 2,500 years ahead of its time.

The Phaistos Disk is a small clay disk recovered during a dig at Phaistos, the site of an ancient Minoan palace on the south coast of Crete. About 6.5 inches (16.5 cm) across and 0.5 inches (1 cm) thick, it is inscribed on both sides with spiral patterns of symbols and lines, with the latter grouping the former into boxes, apparently separating the symbols into words. The disk was found in 1908 by Italian archaeologist Luigi Pernier, along with several clay tablets, but there was something extremely special about this find. It had been deliberately fired (the process by which soft clay is baked hard, giving permanence to marks made on it), unlike the clay tablets usually found in Minoan palaces, which were only baked when the palaces in which they had been kept or discarded burned down.

But what is truly extraordinary is that it had been printed using the technology of block printing, in which specially carved stamps are pressed into the wet clay. Judging by the layer in which it was found and the other items buried alongside it, the disk has been confidently dated to about 1700 BCE, yet the technology of block printing is not known anywhere else in the world until it appeared in China in the 9th century CE, 2,500 years later! Even more strangely, the hieroglyphs on the disk do not belong to any known writing system, and debate rages over whether they even resemble any contemporary scripts (see below), making the Phaistos Disk instantly mysterious because it is incomprehensible.

Above: View of Side A of the Phaistos Disc, showing the text spiraling into (or out from) the center.

READING THE DISK

As one of the great mysteries of Bronze Age archaeology, the Phaistos Disk has inspired a bewildering array of interpretations and translations. The "writing" on the disk is in the form of pictograms and symbols resembling hieroglyphs. It is arranged in a line that spirals in clockwise from the outer edge of the disk to the center, or the other way round, although the fact that the symbols seem to be more squashed together in the center suggests that someone began printing it from the outside and started to run out of space toward the center. The vertical lines between groups of symbols are generally assumed to be word dividers, and although there are 241 characters (divided into 61 "words") on the disk, many are repeated, so that only 45 different glyphs or symbols are present. This is probably too many to be an alphabet (where each symbol equates to one letter or sound), but too few to be an ideographic script (where each symbol represents a whole word), so it is generally accepted that the signs are syllables, such as *ka-* or *ki-*, perhaps with some ideograms too.

OTHER MINOAN SCRIPTS

The three other scripts found in ancient Minoan remains are Linear A, Linear B, and Cretan hieroglyphic. Both Linear scripts use similar symbols, but encode for different languages. The language written down with Linear A has never been deciphered and so Linear A inscriptions cannot be read, but Linear B was deciphered in 1953 and shown to be an early form of Greek. Cretan hieroglyphic pre-dates both the Linear scripts but is known from relatively few instances and cannot be deciphered, although some signs seem to be plain enough, since they depict commodities such as sheep, sometimes with numbers next to them. The conventional view is the Phaistos Disk script resembles none of the other Minoan scripts and is completely unique, meaning that only these 45 symbols are available to scholars, making it impossible to decipher. For instance, in his 1990 book The *Phaistos Disc— the Enigma of an Aegean Script*, Louis Godart argues "there are no definite comparisons between the signs of the disk and the syllabograms of the three known Cretan scripts (Hieroglyphs, Linear A, and Linear B) . . ."

But not everyone agrees. Some scholars argue that there are clear similarities between some of the Phaistos symbols and symbols from Linear A and Cretan hieroglyphic. For instance, the object known as the Arkalochori Axe, a decorative double axe or

Above: A line drawing of Side B of the Phaistos Disk; vertical lines appear to divide the script into words.

"labrys" found in 1934 on Crete and dated to the 2nd millennium BCE, is inscribed with signs, some of which might be said to resemble Linear A and some Phaistos Disk symbols. Some of the more typical ancient Minoan tablets found at Phaistos can also be interpreted as sharing some symbols with the disk. Similarities between some Linear A symbols and Phaistos ones have led to the suggestion that the Phaistos script is simply a more decorative elaboration of Linear A, although this does not help to translate it.

CALENDAR OR BOARD GAME?

There may also be similarities between the Phaistos symbols and other contemporary or near-contemporary Bronze Age Mediterranean writing, leading to interpretations of the Phaistos text in terms of Egyptian hieroglyphics, Hieroglyphic Luwian, and proto-Byblic script. Star map, teaching aid, magical curse, religious ritual, proof of a geometric theorem, prayer—these are all among the many interpretations of the Phaistos Disk. Ideas considered more plausible by mainstream archaeology include that the disk is a calendar, or possibly even a board game. For instance, "chase"

Below: The Arkalochori Axe, which may offer the best opportunity to identify some of the Phaistos Disk script.

games, in which game pieces chase each other along a board like today's Snakes and Ladders, are known from the Bronze Age, and the ancient Egyptians, who interacted heavily with the Minoans, had a board game called Mehen, "the coiled one," which might link to the spiral nature of the text on the disk. Such ancient game boards were often two-sided, just like the disk.

A FORGERY AND A JOKE

In 1999 Jerome Eisenberg, an American art historian, art dealer, and expert on ancient forgeries, suggested the whole affair was a hoax. Writing to *The Economist*, he argued, "In my opinion, having studied the Phaistos Disk at length some 30 years ago, the reason it has not been deciphered and that its symbols do not relate in any way whatsoever to any other known script is simple: it is a forgery. It is a joke perpetrated by a clever archaeologist [Pernier] from the Italian mission to Crete upon his fellow excavators." Pernier's motive was to compete with contemporary headline-grabbing discoveries of Arthur Evans at Knossos.

Eisenberg argues that Crete's Heraklion Archaeological Museum could settle the issue by doing a thermoluminescence test, which reveals when an object was last heated; he says this would probably "date the firing of the clay at about 100 years ago . . . [solving] the mystery of the disk." The reluctance of the museum to do so, Eisenberg argues, shows that they prefer to maintain the hoax as the disk generates attention and income for them, although an alternative point of view is that thermoluminescence testing requires a lot of material and might incur significant damage to the artifact. If the disk is a forgery, resemblances between Phaistos symbols and other Minoan writing might be because Pernier used real sources to inspire his fake, but epigraphic scholar Brian Colless points out that the Arkalochori Axe was discovered after the disk yet seems to bear similarities: "The fact remains that the Phaistos script is represented on other documents from Phaistos, and so the forgery hypothesis is unnecessary . . ."

— FAR OUT — THEORIES

Assuming it is genuine, the real mystery of the Phaistos Disk is the apparent anachronism of the technology that created it. For proponents of the ancient astronaut hypothesis, the disk is a classic example of a technology "out of time," and hence striking evidence for the intervention of an advanced extraterrestrial civilization in the Bronze Age world. But invoking "space gods" is entirely unnecessary to explain the one-off nature of the disk. Historian Jared Diamond uses the disk as proof that the march of technological progress is not smooth, unidirectional, and irreversible: apparently it is possible to "uninvent" something.

Above: The B side of the Disk; a product that perhaps couldn't find a market, and so disappeared for over 2,000 years.

Despite the significant amount of effort and expertise that went into creating the wood blocks to print the disk, not to mention devising the script they record, the artifact remains unique. The vast majority of Bronze Age people were illiterate, so perhaps handwritten scripts such as Linear A and B served well enough the limited needs of the tiny number of literate scribes; block printing was too expensive and laborious to be economically or culturally viable, so that the technology was discarded and of the few instances of its use only one has survived.

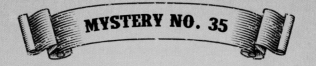

THE ARK OF THE COVENANT

Date: *ca.* 623 BCE
Location: Jerusalem, Israel

A wooden and gold box with strange powers was the most holy artifact of the ancient Jews, before it mysteriously disappeared.

The Ark of the Covenant (*aron ha-berit* in Hebrew), also known as the Ark of the Testimony and the Ark of the Lord, was the chest in which were kept the original stone Tablets of Law that Moses brought down from Mount Sinai. Built according to specifications dictated by God himself, it was an artifact of terrible power and awesome presence, sometimes appearing to have a will of its own. Its disappearance is one of the great mysteries of biblical history, and there have been numerous, though often suspect and ideologically motivated, claims to have tracked it down.

The Ark is the most holy piece of furniture ever made. According to the book of Exodus, God commanded Moses to build a chest, or ark, in which to house the Tablets of Law inscribed with the Ten Commandments, and gave very specific instructions: it was to be two and a half cubits long, and a cubit and a half wide and high. At the time of Moses, the cubit in question was probably

the royal cubit of Egypt, which was 21 inches (53 cm), making the Ark 4 feet 4 inches (1.3 m) long and 2 feet 7 inches (76 cm) wide and deep—roughly the size of a coffee table. God instructed that the Ark was to be constructed from setim wood (aka shittim wood), an expensive and durable kind of acacia, covered on both sides with gold, with a band of gold around the rim. Two rods of gold-covered settim fitted into sets of golden rings on each side of the chest, allowing the ancient Hebrews to carry the Ark with them on their wanderings, and when they stopped and made camp they followed more divine instructions in setting up a tent shrine known as the Tabernacle or Sanctuary. The Tabernacle was a frame of planks and pillars of settim wood, with fixtures of brass, silver, and gold, draped with fabrics of linen, goat hair, and leather. It could be dismantled and used to help pack the Ark.

Above: An early 16th-century Italian painting showing King David bringing the Ark to Jerusalem.

The most striking element of the Ark was the *kapporet* or cover, known as the Mercy Seat in later traditions. It was made of solid gold, cast into a plate from which projected two cherubims. These are not to be confused with the chubby babies of later eras; in the ancient Near East, cherubim were terrifying human–animal hybrids that mediated divine power, and the cherubim of the cover of the Ark probably resembled winged sphinxes, with their wings outstretched, nearly touching.

The Ark was constructed to hold the Tablets of Law, but other items were supposed to be placed in the Tabernacle, and possibly in the Ark itself: a golden vessel of manna from heaven, and the rod of Aaron, which had undergone miraculous transformation. Placed either in or alongside the Ark was a book of Law written by Moses. When the Tabernacle was finally superseded by the Temple of Solomon, the innermost sanctum, known as the Holy of Holies, was constructed along the same lines. According to the book of Kings, by this time the Ark contained only the Tablets.

Above: Cherubim on a replica of the Ark of the Covenant.

POWER AND PRESENCE

The Bible records various manifestations of supernatural power by the Ark. Sometimes a mist or cloud appeared in the space between the wings of the cherubim on the Mercy Seat, and this was said to be the divine presence; and in some passages it seems to be God himself manifesting there, for God would speak directly to Moses from the lid of the Ark. This fits in with other passages in which God seems to identify himself as being one and the same as the Ark. The Ark was carried by the Hebrews and later by the Israelites when they went on campaign or into battle, and it inspired terror in their adversaries. The Ark helped topple the walls of Jericho, and when it was captured by the Philistines and taken to their camp it brought down upon them plague and woe, until they returned it. It could glow and give off sparks, consume with fire those who displeased it, and strike down dead anyone who dared to touch it, as in the tale of the

Above: An 1860 chromolithograph showing Joshua wielding the Ark to effect the fall of Jericho.

unfortunate Uzzah, who reached out to stop the Ark from toppling over as it was carried in procession, and was killed on the spot. When the Ark was placed in the Holy of Holies, the book of Kings records, a "cloud filled the House of the Lord . . . for the glory of the Lord filled the House of God."

In the Bible, the Ark was created in the year of the Exodus from Egypt. The traditional chronology of Exodus is drawn from a passage in the book of Kings, which states that the Exodus happened 480 years before Solomon built the Temple, Solomon himself being dated by correspondence with a contemporaneous Egyptian pharaoh mentioned in the Bible. This dates the construction of the Ark to 1446 BCE, although many scholars dispute the historicity of the Exodus, and others argue that 1250 BCE is a more realistic date.

After its years of wandering and being kept in the Tabernacle, King David made plans to house the Ark in a magnificent temple to be constructed in his new capital at Jerusalem, gathering materials to that effect, but the actual construction of the Temple was left to his successor, Solomon. In 966 BCE, according to the conventional biblical chronology, the Ark moved into its new home, which remained its base for at least 300 years. During this time it was taken out to be carried on military campaigns or in processions, and occasionally to be protected and hidden from wicked kings. *Second Chronicles* provides the last biblical mention of the Ark, recording that King Josiah ordered it to be brought back to the Temple. The dates for Josiah's reign are considered to be firmly established, giving a reliable date for the last mention of the Ark: 623 BCE. What happened to the Ark after this is one of the great mysteries of history.

The most plausible explanation is that it was carried off or destroyed by one of the succession of invaders and despoilers who conquered and/or sacked Jerusalem, most notably the destruction of the First Temple during the Babylonian conquest of 586 BCE. Nebuchadnezzar took Jerusalem, devastated the Temple, and forced the Jews into exile in Babylon, and it was common practice for the idols and artifacts of conquered people to be carted off as well, to be installed in the sacred precinct of Babylon as vassals of the dominant Babylonian gods. The Bible records the construction of the Second Temple 70 years later, but the Ark is not mentioned. When the Romans conquered Jerusalem in 70 CE, according to the Romano-Jewish historian Josephus, the victorious general Titus found that the Second Temple's Holy of Holies was empty. Friezes depicting the Roman conquest of Jerusalem clearly show artifacts being looted from the Temple, but the Ark is not among them.

There are traditions in the Talmud, the books of commentary on Jewish law and lore, suggesting that the Ark was hidden away, possibly by Josiah in expectation of the imminent Babylonian conquest. Modern theories about its resting place and claims to have located it rest on the belief that the Ark was hidden in a tunnel or cave under the Temple Mount, or perhaps in a cave overlooking the Dead Sea. The prophet Jeremiah is said to have hidden the Ark in a cave on Mount Nebo, now on the Jordanian side of the Dead Sea. The Copper Scroll, an extraordinary treasure map that forms part of the Dead Sea Scrolls find, discusses sacred artifacts from the Temple hidden in a similar location. Other suggested hiding places for the Ark include the Hill of Tara in Ireland, the Ka'ba in Mecca, and the state of Utah in the US.

— FAR OUT —
THEORIES

Suggested as early as 1915, by Serbian-American electrical inventor Nikola Tesla, is the theory that the Ark was a giant Leyden jar—a capacitor or device for storing electrical charge, not officially invented until 1747. A Leyden jar has conductors, insulators, and negative and positive terminals, and there are parallels between the design and phenomena associated with Leyden jars and those of the Ark and the Tabernacle. The wooden parts of the Ark could be the insulators and the gold parts the conductors, with the cherubim acting as the terminals. The drapes of the Tabernacle would act to charge the capacitor through rubbing, as a balloon gets charged by rubbing against a woolen sweater. The narrow gap between the wings of the cherubim might lead to coronal discharges (glows) and ionization of the air, seeding droplet formation for mists and clouds, while sudden discharge of the charge stored in a Leyden jar as big as the Ark would be more than sufficient to kill a man. The poles, which were never to be removed, might have helped the Hebrews carry the Ark without being electrocuted.

Above: Nikola Tesla, pictured on a Serbian banknote. Tesla was one of those who suggested that the Ark might have been an electrical technology.

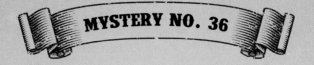

THE BAGHDAD BATTERY

Date: *ca.* 200 BCE?
Location: Baghdad, Iraq

An ancient Persian jar is discovered, but it is soon clear that it resembles a battery, despite pre-dating conventionally recognized electrochemical technology by at least 1,200 years.

The Baghdad Battery is an artifact of uncertain provenance and function, which has become a mainstay of the alternative archaeology universe, because it resembles an electrochemical battery. The battery was not "officially" invented until 1799, when Alessandro Volta piled up discs of zinc and copper or silver, interleaved with cardboard disks soaked in brine, to create the Voltaic pile. But the discovery of a small jar, apparently dating back to *ca.* 200 BCE, suggests that in fact this honor might belong to the ancient Parthians, 2,000 years earlier.

The story of the Baghdad Battery depends entirely on the reports of the German director of the National Museum of Iraq, Wilhelm König. In 1940 he wrote an article about a curious jar, which he said had been dug up in the village of Khujut Rabu, just outside Baghdad, in 1938. It is not clear whether König had excavated the jar himself, been present at the time, or simply come across

the artifact in the archives of the museum—the kind of uncertain provenance that raises a red flag to skeptics. According to König, the jar had been found in the lower layers of a site associated with the ancient Parthians (who ruled Persia from *ca.* 250 BCE–225 CE), and hence he dated it to around 200 BCE.

Above: Alessandro Volta (1745–1827), demonstrating his electricity-generating apparatus to Napoleon.

KÖNIG'S CONCLUSIONS

The object was a small, fat, clay jar, about 5 inches (13 cm) tall. Stuffed down the neck of the jar was a copper cylinder about 3.5 inches (9 cm) tall and 1 inch (2.5 cm) across, made of a rolled sheet of beaten copper with a separate base crimped onto the bottom and sealed with asphalt. Inside the copper cylinder was a heavily corroded iron jar. The whole assemblage was fixed into the neck of the jar by an asphalt plug. To König, the resemblance to a battery was self-evident, and his argument was strengthened when acidic residue was found coating the inside of the jar. The case seemed proven: the ancient Persians had created a crude battery, with iron and copper electrodes in an acidic electrolyte (probably lemon juice, vinegar, or simply grape juice).

ANCIENT ELECTROPLATING

But to what end? König was familiar with ancient Persian objects that were gilded or silvered, which is to say decorated with a thin layer of gold or silver. A battery generating current would make electroplating possible, where an infinitesimally thin film of a precious metal is deposited onto the surface of a cheaper one. König's contention seemed to be backed up by subsequent studies. After World War II, an American engineer built a replica of the "Battery," filled it with grape juice, and showed that it generated a small but measurable current of about a volt. On its own this would be insufficient for any useful purpose, but maybe several such jars connected in series would pack enough punch, and in fact it seems that König had identified around a dozen of the jars—a group of "Baghdad Batteries." In 1978, German researcher Dr. Arne Eggebrecht claimed to have constructed just such a series, and to have used it for electroplating just as König suggested.

THE CASE AGAINST THE BATTERY

But here the story begins to turn sour. A researcher at the institute where Eggebrecht worked could find no record of the experiments nor anyone who remembered them. Skeptics have since pointed out major flaws in König's interpretation. Firstly, the Baghdad Battery closely resembles pottery of the Sassanian era (225–640 CE), suggesting that it probably dates to around 800 years later than believed. Secondly, if it is a battery, the object has major design flaws: the copper tube should be open, not sealed, to allow oxygen to reach the electrolyte, or the current-carrying potential of the small quantity of electrolyte within the sealed cylinder would quickly be exhausted. To function as a battery, the jar would need to have metal wires, but the asphalt plug seems to mitigate against the presence of such wires and there is no evidence that any wires were associated with the object. Even if wires were present, the jar would make a very inefficient and feeble battery; more electrical current can be generated by sticking two metal probes into a lemon. Thirdly, none of the gilded or silvered objects known from

— FAR OUT —
THEORIES

One potential use for an ancient battery might have been to produce tiny shocks or at least mild sensations, for instance if concealed within a metal idol. Ancient temples are widely suspected to have used tricks and devices to have entertained, impressed, and awed worshippers. Alternatively, mild currents could have been used for medical electro-therapy; the ancients were said to have used electric eels for this purpose—why not batteries? For adherents of the ancient astronauts theory, the Baghdad Battery is yet another example of an out-of-time technology that can only be explained as a gift from the space gods.

Above: A shrine at the ancient city of Hatra, an Arab city under Parthian control in the 2nd century BCE.

ancient Persia appear to have been electroplated; their manufacture can be explained solely using the known methods. Fourthly, similar objects are known from elsewhere in ancient Persia, and they appear to have been containers for sacred scrolls of papyrus or bronze.

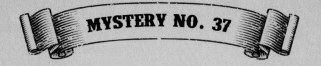

THE ANTIKYTHERA MECHANISM

Date: *ca.* 80 BCE
Location: Antikythera, near Crete

In 1900, divers in the Aegean Sea discovered an ancient astronomical computer of remarkable sophistication; this simple find has since rewritten the history of technology.

In 1900, a party of sponge divers from Syme, sheltering from a storm, discovered the remains of a wooden shipwreck perched on a ledge in waters around 165 feet (50 m) deep off the island of Antikythera, near the northwest tip of Crete. One of the oldest wrecks ever found, it was of a 1st-century BCE Roman cargo ship, since described as the *Titanic* of the Classical world thanks to the extraordinary wealth of artifacts and treasure it contained.

What followed was perhaps the first underwater archaeological operation, and given the depth, primitive technology available, and extreme danger for divers, it was a messy affair. The journalist and underwater archaeologist Peter Throckmorton described it in 1970: "It was . . . as if the tomb of Tutankhamen had been excavated in five-minute shifts by drunken stevedores who had never seen an Egyptian tomb, working in semi-darkness, dressed in American football pads with coal scuttles on their heads."

TREASURES OF THE DEEP

Nonetheless, the divers salvaged some incredible pieces: bronze and marble sculpture, large numbers of coins, pottery, and amphorae, Alexandrian glass, a bronze bedstead ornamented with the heads of animals, and the "Antikythera Youth," an ancient Greek bronze statue of a nude. Yet the most important and valuable find perhaps looked the least impressive: a lump of rock and barnacles from which projected a small piece of bronze. Labeled Item 15087, packaged up, and sent off to the National Museum of Greece, its full significance was not appreciated for another two years, when an archaeologist reviewing the finds realized that it had once been part of a wooden frame, and contained pieces of bronze fused together. Closer inspection revealed extraordinary features, including fine, triangular-toothed gear wheels and a dial, and other related pieces were identified, which bore inscriptions in ancient Greek. Item 15087 appeared

Above: The largest piece of the Antikythera Mechanism contains 27 of the device's gears, including the largest, the primary gear.

to be the remains of some sort of ancient clockwork device: the Antikythera Mechanism.

Initially, it was believed that the mechanism was an early form of astrolabe, a device a bit like a slide rule, which aids in the calculation of the motions of heavenly bodies and can help work out dates, latitudes, and similar information. The suggestion that it might be a more sophisticated clockwork calculator was dismissed, because the earliest mechanical astronomical calculator known at this point was the "Box of the Moon," a device with eight gear wheels constructed by the Islamic astronomer al-Biruni in the early 11th century. More complex clockwork was thought to be the preserve of the period after the Scientific Revolution, when it was possible to engineer intricate gears to complement new mathematical comprehension of the complex epicycles of the celestial bodies. It is only recently, after decades of study and the application in 2006 of hi-tech computerized tomography imaging technology by a team from Cardiff University in Wales, that the full picture of the mechanism has emerged.

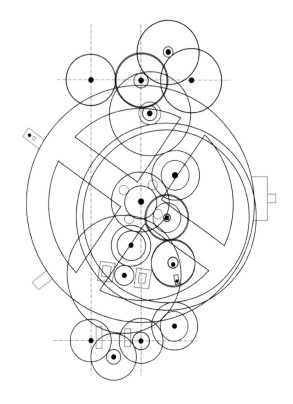

Above: A schematic diagram of the Antikythera Mechanism, showing its many shafts and gears.

ANCIENT ORRERY

It is now understood that the Antikythera Mechanism is a highly sophisticated astronomical calculator or orrery. It could be set using the dials on the faces, and operated by turning a handle to power its 37 gears. These would interact to drive at least seven dials showing movements of celestial bodies, a rotating black

Above: A reconstruction of the mechanism at the Museum of Science, Boston; note the crank on the side.

and silver ball showing phases of the Moon, and dials showing calendrical dates and lunar and solar eclipses. The mechanism could allow for leap years and predict eclipses; it may even have been able to cope with epicycles (circles within circles), a mathematical and technical feat that troubled Isaac Newton in the 18th century. Inscriptions deciphered from the parts show that it was probably made in 82 BCE and had been set to display data from 80 BCE, strongly suggesting a date for the sinking of the ship.

MYSTERIES OF THE MECHANISM

By a wide margin, then, the Antikythera Mechanism is the most sophisticated technological artifact known from antiquity, and raises several questions. Where did it come from? Who made it? Why has nothing else like it ever been seen? When similar devices appeared in Europe in the 17th and 18th centuries, they helped trigger and drive the Scientific and Industrial Revolutions, so perhaps the greatest mystery posed by the mechanism is why, given the extraordinary technical ingenuity, engineering ability, and theoretical accomplishment that was clearly available at the time, didn't antiquity experience a scientific revolution of its own?

The evidence from the Antikythera wreck suggests that the ship had collected booty and trophies from Asia Minor (specifically the recently defeated city-state Pergamum) and the Ionian islands, including Rhodes, and was on its way back to Rome. Rhodes was well known in the ancient world as the home of great philosophers. The Roman writer Cicero wrote an account of a machine that sounds similar to the mechanism, which he attributed to the philosopher Posidonius, who had a workshop in Rhodes in the 1st century BCE; perhaps Posidonius was the creator of the machine? Another candidate is the philosopher and astronomer Hipparchos, also of 1st-century BCE Rhodes. James Evans, an historian of astronomy at the University of Puget Sound in Tacoma, Washington, has linked the astronomical knowledge displayed in the mechanism to Babylonian models, and argues that Hipparchos was known for his work reconciling the Greek and Babylonian modes of mathematics. Possibly one of these men had built the mechanism as a curio for a wealthy Roman—perhaps even Cicero himself?

The degree of technical accomplishment displayed by the mechanism is a clear argument that it cannot have been a one-off, but would more likely have been the product of experienced designers and craftsmen. So why are there no other devices like it? The most obvious explanation is that bronze was rare and valuable (often used to make coins), so that at some point in history such devices were inevitably broken up, melted down, and recycled. Most bronze artifacts known from antiquity have been found, like the mechanism, underwater, where they had been safe from the hands of those who would rework them. In other words, the only reason the Antikythera Mechanism survived is that it sank to a depth of 165 feet (50 m) and lay hidden for 2,000 years.

THE REVOLUTION WOULD NOT BE MECHANIZED

As to the question of why there was no industrial or machine revolution in antiquity, as a result of the theoretical and technical hinterland for which the Mechanism constitutes evidence, the answer seems to lie in the nature of the Classical social economy. The mechanism is not the only remarkable invention known from antiquity. Ancient writings preserve the memory of the hydraulic organ, metal springs, water clock, and force pump invented by

— FAR OUT —
THEORIES

As the ultimate out-of-time technology, the Antikythera Mechanism has prompted far-fetched speculation about ancient astronauts and even time travelers. But for all that it is startlingly unique, the mechanism fits squarely within the known tradition of ancient Greek astronomy. It represents the acme of that tradition, and is of invaluable use to archaeologists and historians in setting a new and exciting benchmark, showing the heights that ancient ingenuity could attain.

Above: The ancient Greek philosopher and astronomer Hipparchos, who may have helped create the Antikythera Mechanism.

Ktesibios of Alexandria in the 3rd century BCE, or the steam engine that could open temple doors and the coin-operated vending machine for holy water, invented by Hero of Alexandria in the 1st century CE. But like the mechanism, these devices were seen as curios; executive toys for the amusement of the elite. The capitalist mechanisms for connecting inventors to markets did not exist, so there was no economic incentive for inventions to be taken up, proliferated, and applied. The ancient writer Suetonius tells the story that an inventor around 70 CE displayed to a Roman emperor a machine that could move columns, only to be dismissed with the objection that such labor-saving devices would cause the poor to starve by robbing them of employment.

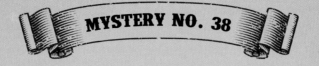

THE TURIN SHROUD

Date: 14th century
Location: Turin, Italy

A linen cloth imprinted with an image of a mutilated human figure is claimed to be the burial shroud of Jesus, and despite evidence suggesting it is a medieval painting, mysteries remain about the formation of the image.

The Shroud of Turin is a 14.5 foot (4.4 m) long, 4 foot (1.13 m) wide strip of linen cloth bearing the front and back images of a man with his hands crossed over his loins. He has long hair and appears to bear the marks of torture and crucifixion, together with many bloodstains. Since 1578 the shroud has been kept in Turin Cathedral and occasionally put on display; the Catholic Church makes no formal statement regarding its authenticity, regarding it simply as an object of veneration. Modern fascination with the shroud dates to the publication of photographs taken in 1898 and 1931, which show that the image revealed in a photographic negative is much more striking than the faint marks visible with the naked eye.

The study of the Turin Shroud—particularly by those who believe in its authenticity—is known as sindology, from the word *sindone*,

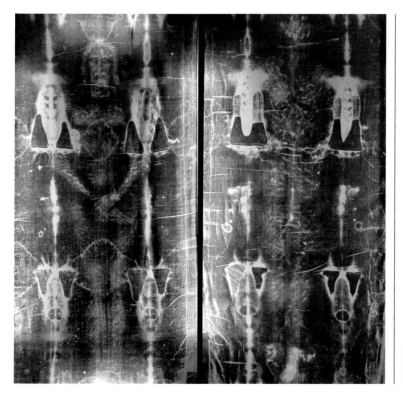

Left: Negative images of the front and back of the Turin Shroud.

denoting the linen cloth used to wrap a dead body. Sindology has evolved into a complex stew of faith, science, history, and rhetoric; one of the most remarkable features of research into and discussion of the shroud is the exchange of claim and counter-claim between skeptics and sindologists. Sindologists believe that the image of Jesus was imprinted on the cloth through processes natural (sweating and bleeding), paranormal (a burst of radiation emitted at the moment of the Resurrection), or supernatural.

The earliest record of the shroud dates to 1355, when it was displayed in a chapel at Lirey, in France. In 1453 Margaret de Charny sold the cloth to the Dukes of Savoy, and it was under their stewardship that the shroud became famous as the actual burial shroud of Jesus. Tracing any provenance for the shroud prior to 1355 is difficult, although it is widely identified with the

Mandylion (the Image of Edessa), a sacred cloth bearing Jesus's face, kept in the holy city of Edessa (now known as Şanliurfa in Turkey, near the border with Syria) from the early centuries CE until 944, when it was transferred to Constantinople, from where it disappeared in 1203.

PUBLIC IMAGES

It is important to note that the shroud and the Mandylion fit within a larger tradition of Christian relics known as *acheiropoietos* (from the Greek for "made without hands"), spontaneously appearing images of which there have been numerous examples. A parallel tradition to the shroud is that of the Sudarium (cloth for wiping the face) or Veronica ("true image"), names given to cloths said to bear the miraculous imprint of the face of Christ, either when he wiped his face during his procession with the cross, or from the cloth used to bind his head after death. In fact, the gospel accounts of Jesus's body being prepared for burial are problematic for sindologists, because they specify that his head was wound with a separate cloth from that used for his body, whereas the image on the shroud corresponds to use of a single cloth for both.

SCIENTIFIC FINDINGS

In 1978, a scientific dimension was added to the shroud mystery with the work of the Shroud of Turin Research Project (STURP). The STURP team used tape to lift fibers and residues from the shroud, and these were subjected to a range of tests. Some

Below: *Saint Veronica with the Veil,* by Mattia Preti, between 1655 and 1660, showing the saint bearing a Veronica.

of the samples were passed to respected American micro-analyst Walter McCrone, whose analysis was devastating to sindology. He claimed to have found pigments of ocher from the body image and vermilion from the bloodstains, apparently proving that the image had been painted. The STURP team, many of whom had become convinced sindologists, strongly refuted McCrone's findings. It was later claimed that analysis proved that the blood was real human blood, type AB, although this itself is widely disputed and it is believed most likely that findings of blood are false positives caused by traces of collagen from rabbit-skin glue, a common ingredient in tempera, used as a binding pigment in medieval painting.

The most high-profile scientific finding was the 1988 radiocarbon dating study. A cloth sample from outside the image was divided in three and sent to labs in Oxford, Tucson, and Zurich, where the samples were cleaned and dated. The three labs found, with a 95 percent confidence range, that the date when the flax for the linen was harvested was between 1260 and 1390. Sindologists have attacked this study ever since; the most common refutation is that the sample was taken from cloth added to repair the shroud following a fire (it was heavily damaged by fire in the 16th century), or that it was contaminated. In fact, the sample was taken from the original linen, and it would take twice as much contaminant as sample to skew the date from the 1st century CE to the 13th century. Although they did not make the link themselves, several of the STURP findings point to the presence of heavy traces of gesso, a sealant layer applied to medieval linens to prepare them for painting, and of plant gums containing red pigment, again suggestive of painted cloths in medieval times.

Above: A negative image of the face from the Turin Shroud, with what look like blood stains from scalp injuries—caused by a crown of thorns?

Another prominent claim by sindologists is that tape-lifted samples show the presence of pollen from plant species found only around Jerusalem. However, the samples in question were supplied by Max Frei, infamous for his role in the Hitler Diaries forgery, and the team who identified the pollen also claim to have spotted previously unnoticed impressions of characteristic Jerusalem-area flora on the Shroud, though to most observers these are invisible.

EASTER PROP

The case against the authenticity of the shroud is crushing. When it first appeared in the 14th century, the Bishop of Troyes, Henry of Poitiers, was tasked with investigating it. He reported that the shroud was a painted cloth, and even tracked down the artist responsible. The chapel at Lirey was allowed to display the shroud on condition that it was advertised as not genuine. Later the artifact may have been associated with miracles, and so it became an object of veneration in its own right, but even after the Dukes of Savoy started to promote its claims to authenticity the Vatican was careful not to agree. Both the three-in-one herringbone weave of the linen and the counterclockwise twist of the yarn from which it is woven are characteristic of Western European cloth production in medieval times.

Historian of medieval relics Charles Freeman describes multiple points of similarity between the iconography of the shroud and depictions of Christ from mid-14th century Europe, such as a gory emphasis on blood. He even tracks, via medieval and later depictions of the shroud, the addition of a loincloth to the originally nude image on the shroud, in deference to developing notions of pious modesty in the late 16th century. Freeman convincingly explains the origins of the shroud as a prop in a popular medieval Easter play in which the empty tomb of Christ is visited by various Marys, who are confronted by an angel brandishing a winding cloth on which is shown the image of the tortured Jesus. He is one of many skeptics who point to the crudity

—FAR OUT—
THEORIES

The disparity between the clarity of the positive and negative images of the shroud today has prompted a lot of speculation about its creation through a form of primitive photography. Writers such as Lynn Picknett and Clive Prince have developed an elaborate conspiracy theory in which the image on the modern shroud was created by none other than Leonardo da Vinci, possibly as a self-portrait, using esoteric knowledge of early photographic technology, as part of a subversive mission to infiltrate aspects of heretical Gnostic Christianity into mainstream Catholicism. Skeptics argue that the modern-day appearance of the shroud is exactly what would be expected of a faded, fire- and water-damaged, and repeatedly folded medieval painted linen.

Above: Leonardo da Vinci; parallels have been drawn between da Vinci's features and those of the image on the Shroud.

of the image and the mismatches between the dimensions and layout of the actual image and those that would be expected if it really were somehow imprinted from a genuine corpse.

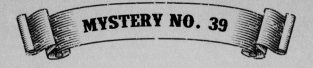

THE VOYNICH MANUSCRIPT

Date: 15th century
Location: Beinecke Rare Book and Manuscript Library, Yale University

The Voynich Manuscript is a medieval book in an indecipherable script; its exotic provenance, otherworldly aura, and stubborn resistance to decoding have made it one of the most enduring challenges in the world of cryptography.

Named for the antiquarian bookseller Wilfred M. Voynich, who acquired it in 1912, this medieval manuscript features colorful botanical and scientific illustrations (described by the library that currently holds the book as "of a provincial but lively character, in ink with washes in various shades of green, brown, yellow, blue, and red") and appears to be a scientific or magical text. It seems to be divided into six sections including ones covering botany, astronomy or astrology, and human reproductive biology, although whether these topics are allegorical is unclear (sex, for instance, was often used as an allegory for alchemical processes such as combination, reaction, separation, and purification). The text is written in a distinctive flowing style and seems to be a cipher, although debate rages on whether it encodes a real language, a made-up one, or none at all.

THE QUEEN'S SORCERER

The manuscript first appears in the historical record when it was sold to Emperor Rudolph II of Germany, the Holy Roman Emperor, in the 1580s. Rudolph was fascinated with all things occult and esoteric, and made his capital at Prague a hotbed of alchemists, magicians, natural philosophers, and con men. Circumstantial evidence strongly suggests the Emperor bought the manuscript from Dr. John Dee, an English scholar, astrologer, mathematician, cryptologist, diplomat, magician, royal counselor, and occasional spy.

Dee was a fascinating character, often described as "Queen Elizabeth's Sorcerer," who drew up astrological charts for royalty, wrote landmark works on cryptography, believed he could communicate with angels through a crystal ball, and embarked on a breathtakingly dangerous mission to Prague to pass on religious admonishments to the Holy Roman Emperor, apparently delivered by Dee's angelic interlocutors. Dee was also a bibliophile who amassed one of the largest private libraries in Europe, and he took many books with him on his voyage to Bohemia.

Below: Pages from the Voynich Manuscript, now held by the Beinecke Rare Book & Manuscript Library, Yale University.

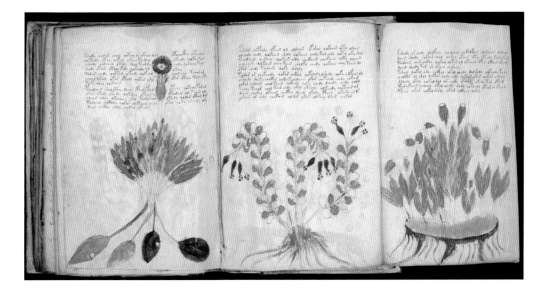

A letter placed within the Voynich
Manuscript records that Emperor
Rudolph paid 600 gold ducats
(equivalent to nearly $100,000 in
modern terms) for the book, believing
it to be the work of the 13th-century
English friar and pioneering natural
philosopher Roger Bacon (known
as Doctor Mirabilis for his exploits
in science, alchemy, and magic).
Dee was said to own several Bacon
manuscripts, and his own records
show that he had 630 ducats while
in Bohemia in October 1586.
Furthermore, Dee's son reported that
while in Bohemia his father owned
"a booke . . . containing nothing butt
Hieroglyphicks, which booke his
father bestowed much time upon: but I could not heare that hee
could make it out."

Above: Dr. John Dee,
whose son recorded his
unsuccessful attempts to
decipher the manuscript.

UNFLAGGING TOIL

A concealed inscription in the manuscript, visible only with
ultraviolet light, records the name Jacobi de Tepenecz, suggesting
that Rudolph passed the book to Jacobus Horcicky de Tepenec,
the imperial pharmacist and keeper of the royal gardens.
Tepenec was a concoctor of plant remedies who had earned
the imperial favor by curing Rudolph of a disease before going
on to make a fortune from his elixirs; Rudolph owed him
money, and the book may well have appealed to his botanical
and pharmaceutical interests. From Tepenec, the manuscript
passed to Prague alchemist Georg Baresch, who would spend
decades trying to decipher it. An appeal for help from the Jesuit
polymath Athanasius Kircher, then famous for his claims to have
translated Egyptian hieroglyphs, had encouraged Baresch to ask

to purchase the volume. In 1666, after Baresch's death, his friend and beneficiary Johannes Marcus Marci of Cronland passed the manuscript on to the Jesuit, noting Baresch's relationship with the tome: "To its deciphering he devoted unflagging toil, as is apparent from attempts of his which I send you herewith, and he relinquished hope only with his life." Obsession with cracking the code was already becoming a theme of the manuscript's history.

THE VOYNICH COLLECTION

The Manuscript remained in the possession of the Jesuits for nearly 250 years, although attacks on the order led to it being hidden away. In 1912 it was discovered in the archives of the Jesuit College at the Villa Mondragone, in Frascati, near Rome, by Wilfred Voynich. Voynich was another colorful character—a Russian revolutionary who had decamped to London and set up an antiquarian bookshop as a front for his agitation, along with his wife Ethel Boole, a novelist and daughter of the famous mathematician. In 1969, the manuscript was donated to the Beinecke Library at Yale, but by this time it had already cast its spell over the new global community of cryptanalysts that had sprung up in the wake of World War II. Voynich himself had passed the book to cryptographer William Newbold, a professor of philosophy at the University of Pennsylvania, hoping that he would decipher it and prove that it was indeed a work by Roger Bacon. Newbold spent many years

Below: Roger Bacon with astronomical equipment; Emperor Rudolph believed that Bacon was the original author of the manuscript.

poring over the most minute details of the script, having deluded himself into believing the key to the cipher lay in minuscule squiggles that were actually an artifact of the aging of the ink but which Newbold believed to be a code in micrographic shorthand.

NEVER DECRYPTED

Newbold's analysis was refuted by William Friedman, the leading cryptanalyst of his day, who arranged a working group to study the manuscript. Friedman and the finest minds in cryptanalysis proved unable to decipher the manuscript, leading Friedman to propose that the Voynich script encoded an artificial or constructed language. The resistance of the text to decipherment, despite the large volume of text available, has convinced many that it is essentially meaningless: a hoax. For instance, cryptographer Klaus Schmeh notes: "There have been numerous encrypted texts since the Middle Ages and 99.9% have been cracked. If you have a whole book, as [with the Voynich Manuscript], it should be 'quite easy' as there is so much material for analysts to work with."

NATURAL OR CONSTRUCTED?

The most likely culprit of a hoax must surely be John Dee or a contemporary; someone who would have known the Emperor would pay handsomely for a mysterious manuscript. But a 2009 radiocarbon analysis showed the calfskin parchment of the manuscript dates to between 1404 and 1438, which both rules out Roger Bacon as the author and also mitigates against a 16th-century forgery, unless such a forger had gone to the trouble of obtaining extremely old parchment, somehow anticipating modern dating technology. Believers in the semantic authenticity of the text point to over 25 studies showing "Voynichese" has statistical similarities to real language.

In 2014 Bedfordshire University's Stephen Bax claimed to have identified ten words as plant names, and to have pinned down the treatise to a Near Eastern or Asian origin. Voynich expert and

—FAR OUT—
THEORIES

Inevitably, the Voynich Manuscript has been adopted by the alternative history community as a kind of all-purpose palimpsest, on which can be projected any and all claims: it is a secret Rosicrucian spellbook, or an extraterrestrial encyclopedia rendered in alien hieroglyphs. A more conventional suggestion that emerged in 2014 was based on supposed resemblance between some of the plants in the manuscript and Mexican flora shown in Aztec codices, such as the xiuhamolli or "soap plant" shown in the 1552 Codex Cruz-Badianus, known as the "Aztec Herbal." This theory, advanced by Arthur Tucker and Rexford Talbert of Delaware State University, argues that the manuscript describes a botanical garden in central Mexico and is mainly written in an extinct dialect of Nahuatl. Voynich skeptic Gordon Rugg,

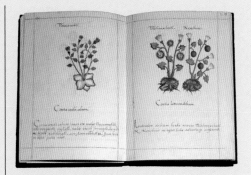

Above: A facsimile of the Codex Cruz-Badianus, which is at least superficially similar to the Voynich Manuscript.

of Keele University in the UK, dismisses this notion, arguing, "If I sat down with a random plant generator software and got it to generate 50 completely fictitious plants, I'm pretty sure I could find 20 real plants that happen to look like 20 of the made-up plants."

blogger Nick Pelling was among several in the Voynich community to refute Bax's claims: "I'm quite certain that every single one of Stephen Bax's conclusions to date have been built upon a long sequence of easily demonstrable mistakes."

FURTHER READING

Aveni, Anthony. *Between the Lines: The Mystery of the Giant Ground Drawings of Ancient Nasca, Peru*. Austin: University of Texas Press, 2000.

Begg, Paul. *Mary Celeste: The Greatest Mystery of the Sea*. London: Routledge, 2006.

Bell, Karl. *The Legend of Spring-Heeled Jack: Victorian Urban Folklore and Popular Cultures*. Suffolk: Boydell Press, 2012.

Berlitz, Charles. *The Bermuda Triangle*. New York City: Doubleday, 1974.

Dash, Mike. *Borderlands*. London: William Heinemann, 1997.

Davies, Paul. *The Eerie Silence: Searching for Ourselves in the Universe*. London: Penguin, 2011.

Diamond, Jared. *Guns, Germs and Steel*. New York City: Vintage, 1998.

Fischer, Steven Roger. *Island at the End of the World: The Turbulent History of Easter Island*. London: Reaktion Books, 2006.

Gray, Geoffrey. *SKYJACK: The Hunt for D. B. Cooper*. New York City: Broadway Books, 2012.

Gray, Robert. *The Elusive Wow: Searching for Extraterrestrial Intelligence*. Chicago: Palmer Square Press, 2011.

Greenwood, Kerry. *Taman Shud: The Somerton Man Mystery*. Kensington: NewSouth Publishing, 2012.

Haag, Michael. *Templars: History and Myth: From Solomon's Temple to the Freemasons*. London: Profile, 2009.

Harpur, Merrily. *Mystery Big Cats. Marlborough: Heart of Albion Press*, 2006.

Harrison, Paul. *The Encyclopaedia of the Loch Ness Monster*. London: Robert Hale, 2000.

Kelly, Saul. *The Hunt for Zerzura: The Lost Oasis and the Desert War*. London: John Murray, 2003.

Leigh, Richard, Michael Baigent, and Henry Lincoln. *The Holy Blood and the Holy Grail*. London: Arrow, 1996.

Levy, Joel. *Atlas of Atlantis and Other Lost Continents*. London: Godsfield Press, 2011.

Marchant, Jo. *Decoding the Heavens: Solving the Mystery of the World's First Computer*. London: Windmill Books, 2009.

McGovern, Una, ed. *Chambers Dictionary of the Unexplained*. London: Chambers Harrap, 2007.

Miller, Lee. *Roanoke: Solving the Riddle of England's Lost Colony*. London: Pimlico, 2001.

Parker Pearson, Mike. *Stonehenge: Exploring the Greatest Stone Age Mystery*. New York City: Simon and Schuster, 2013.

Pelling, Nicholas. *The Curse of the Voynich: The Secret History of the World's Most Mysterious Manuscript*. Surbiton: Compelling Press, 2006.

Pemberton, John. *Conquistadors: Searching for El Dorado, the Terrifying Spanish conquest of the Aztec and Inca Empires*. Austin: Futura, 2011.

Rickard, Bob, and John Michell. *The Rough Guide to Unexplained Phenomena*, 2nd edn. London: Rough Guides, 2007.

Scott-Clark, Catherine, and Adrian Levy. *The Amber Room*. London: Atlantic Books, 2005.

Wilson, Ian. *The Shroud*. New York City: Bantam, 2011.

INDEX

IMAGE CREDITS